VOICE OF CIVILISATION

VOICE OF CIVILISATION

An Enquiry into Advertising

by

DENYS THOMPSON

LONDON
FREDERICK MULLER, LTD.
29 GREAT JAMES STREET, W.C.1

FIRST PUBLISHED BY FREDERICK MULLER, LTD.
IN 1943
PRINTED IN GREAT BRITAIN BY
ROBERT MACLEHOSE AND CO. LTD., GLASGOW

Second Edition 1944
Third Edition 1947

TO MY MOTHER

PREFACE

THIS book seeks to show that advertising is an influence much more powerful than is generally realised ; that it has already had important effects on society; and that we need to examine its results now and watch it closely in future.

As it is often argued that the commercial life of the country could not continue without advertising, the economic case is examined first. Readers who are not interested in this aspect should start at Chapter II.

Thanks are due to H. D. Barnes, L. E. C. Bruce, R. B. Ford, E. Penning-Rowsell, H. E. Poole and my wife for specimens, to Harrods Ltd. for permission to quote in full the advertisement on p. 209, and to the *News-Chronicle* for checking a statement on p. 137.

CONTENTS

CHAPTER I

IT PAYS TO ADVERTISE

I. What is paid

In order to understand the position of advertising in modern industry we must regard it as one indication of the greater emphasis which has been placed on marketing in recent times. The development of advertising is a phenomenon which is intimately associated with the growing complexity of consumption, with the desire of the producer to control his market, with the increasing severity of competition, and finally, with the growth of the large-scale business enterprise.

F. W. TAYLOR, Economics of Advertising

ESTIMATES of the cost of advertising in this country range from £85,000,000 to £200,000,000 annually in the years between 1919 and 1939. During this period the national income was between £5,000,000,000 and £6,000,000,000 a year. For comparison it is worth noting that in 1939 the State spent £52,321,000 on education, and approximately £300,000 on Scientific Investigation and £1,500,000 on Land Fertility (1).

A single advertising agency, J. Walter Thompson, claims to spend £10,000,000 a year on behalf of its clients throughout the world; and more workers (about 18,000) are employed in advertising than in either the chemical or electrical (omitting radio) engineering industry. The lowest estimate mentioned was made by the *Economist* (2), and comprises

Press Advertising	-	£35,000,000
Posters -	-	4,000,000
Direct Mail -	-	25,000,000
Window Display	-	20,000,000
Miscellaneous -	-	1,000,000

In so far as this estimate is not based on exact information, it is probably conservative; posters, for example, are said to account for £7,000,000 a year, according to another authority (3).

A few of the sums stated to have been spent in a year by separate products are: £400,000 for Daily Express Newspapers, £300,000 for Bovril and Oxo together (4), £223,378 (Press only) for bicycles (5), £30,000 for Farmer's Glory wheat flakes (radio only) (5). The Imperial Tobacco Company is said at one time to have spent £20,000 a month on promoting the sale of 'Four Aces' alone, while Carreras were spending £8,000 a month on 'Clubs' (4). Cigarettes claim about £1,000,000 a year; a similar sum is spent on each of the trades in foodstuffs, drinks, soap and toilet goods (6). The cement industry accounts for £100,000 a year (7), and the trade in patent medicines for about £3,000,000—roughly equal to the profits of the papers in which the advertisements appeared (8).

The figures given above are for direct advertising. The indirect methods are of almost equal importance, though it is difficult to say where they end. They include such items as expensive packaging, elaborate catalogues, decorated vans, presents and samples to reporters and others, and 'loss leaders'—price reductions to catch new customers. And the free trips to Somerset and back which a maker of pharmaceutical products offered to medical students in London are probably not an isolated example of the length to which an advertiser will go to buy the favour of key consumers (10). Expenditure, too, on unnecessarily pretentious buildings, imposing commissionaires, large staffs, entertainments, gifts to charities, additions to hospital buildings and so on, can all be reckoned as advertising. Some of these items must account for the fact that insurance companies spend from £26 to £59 for every £100 they collect in premiums.

This enquiry will deal mainly with advertising in the Press, because it accounts for larger sums of money than any other medium, and is likely therefore to have a more marked impact on the public. Here another sub-division can be made to render the subject more tractable; a rough but workable distinction can be made between advertisements which offer information of goods and services for sale, and those the chief aim of which is persuasion. In a newspaper this approximates to the difference between classified and displayed advertisements. The latter of course do sometimes give information, but rarely unmixed with persuasion. A glance at any newspaper brings out the point clearly; the classified advertisements are in type just large enough to be legible, they are aimed at and read by those who have a purpose in reading them. The methods of most displayed advertisements are in sharp contrast; they will be discussed later, and at the moment it need only be said that they are usually aggressive. Among this class are some which set out to persuade by using rational argument and honestly selected figures, but the aim of the majority is to influence the thoughts and actions of a large number of people by inducing them to suspend individual and rational judgment.

Moreover, classified advertisements are in a minority. Though *The Times* over a representative period averaged 941 column inches of classified advertisements to 570 of display, the *Daily Mail*, *Daily Express* and *Daily Herald* carried respectively 39, 104, and 82 column inches of classified matter to 1,554, 1,454 and 1,165 of display, during the same period (11). Another useful form of classified advertisement, which should be developed, is exemplified by book catalogues and the detailed lists of hotels and pensions that used to be issued by the Swedish and Austrian travel bureaux.

Some examples of the rates charged before the 1939 war may be of interest. A whole page of the *News of the World* costs £2,200, the *Daily Mail* front page £1,400; and other figures for whole pages are: *Punch*, £200; *Sunday Pictorial*,

£700; *News-Chronicle*, £700; *Picture Post*, £250 (increased in April, 1939); *Everybody's*, £140; *The Listener*, £50.

II. Whom does it pay?

Continuous and skilful advertising provides an assured and workable means for taxing effective income away from consumers and distributing it among manufacturers who advertise, and newspaper and magazine publishers whose income comes preponderantly from such advertising.

CONSUMERS' RESEARCH (U.S.A.), *General Bulletin*, vol. i, No. 3

Expenditure on this scale needs justifying; so I propose now to outline the case for advertising as made by its supporters, and then to examine the argument.

In the first place, it is claimed for advertising that it cheapens goods. It increases the sale of an article to such an extent that the manufacturer is enabled to exploit more thoroughly the advantages of mass-production. Thus he can pay off more quickly the high initial cost of his plant, and by keeping it working to full capacity, he avoids the costly overheads inevitable when demand is only seasonal; 'no one has yet found an effective alternative to advertising for stimulating and regulating the flow of goods from factory to consumer' (12). A similar claim is made in the article on Advertising in the 14th Edition of the *Encyclopædia Britannica*, but the tone in which the following example is recorded suggests that the control of seasonal fluctuation is not very often achieved:

Another particularly interesting case was the advertising by Murphy Radio to overcome the bugbear of nearly every trade—seasonal slumps. Frank Murphy knew that mass-production on a steady scale was the only method of getting manufacturing costs down to a minimum. Seasonal slumps disorganised the factory, piled up overhead costs, were not fair to the workers.

So he ran an advertising campaign which has become historic. He told the public frankly about his problem. He promised that once a line was introduced it would stay 'put' for the rest of the season. . . . Then he asked the public to buy their sets during the off-season . . . his faith in advertising was justified, and the seasonal dip in the sales curve was lifted (13).

In short, advertising by increasing consumption is said to make it possible to make more goods of the same quality for the same overhead costs; thus the manufacturer can lower retail prices and pass on to the consumer the saving effected by mass-production.

The second function of advertising is to give the public information about new goods and create a demand for them; 'modern advertising justifies itself economically by its function of bringing knowledge of desirable merchandise to the consumer' (14). 'The knowledge that a new typewriter at ten pounds will do all the work that I want of it as well as the machine for which, but for the advertisement, I should have paid twenty, is worth whatever may have been added to the cost of the machine; if, indeed, one can properly say that anything has been added, since the cheaper machine has only been rendered possible by large-scale, standardised production, which in its turn has only been made possible by the wide dissemination of its merits' (15). This function of advertising was perhaps more in evidence a few decades ago than to-day. A writer on advertising (13) shows how the increased use of machinery in the 1880's and 1890's enabled prices to be lowered:

This in turn meant that more people could afford to buy grades of merchandise which had hitherto only been purchasable by the wealthy. But the middle classes had to be told about these things, and the easiest, quickest, and cheapest way of telling them was to advertise.

In recent years the informative side of advertising has been stressed more in connection with foreign and dominions markets than the home trade. An official statement of the Advertising Association in 1941 observes, of the post-war period, that

> The command of markets abroad will be absolutely essential to quick recovery ... the nation ... will have something to work on if, during the period when it is impossible to send merchandise oversea to the former extent, goodwill in British goods is maintained. Products off the market are products forgotten, but buyers can and should be repeatedly reminded of them when they are temporarily unobtainable (12).

Thirdly, it is said that advertising, in the ways we have outlined and by increasing the range of choice, has raised the standard of living. The managing director of Dixon's West End Advertising Agency Ltd. puts the case thus:

> Without the advertiser, civilisation as we know it to-day could not exist. To him we owe all the modern amenities which have made our lives so much fuller and easier than anything enjoyed by our fathers and grandfathers. Advertising ... has brought within the reach of 'the man in the street' a host of luxuries which formerly were available only to the wealthy. The motor-car and wireless are two outstanding examples. It was the power of advertising that made the cheap and efficient motor-car a practical possibility; advertising has brought the radio set into millions of homes. In the development of almost every side of our modern culture advertising has played the leading part. Because of the enterprise and energy of the advertiser we are better fed, better clothed, better housed, better entertained, than any generation that has ever lived upon the earth (13).

The fourth of the advantages which advertising is said to bring us is an improvement in the quality of goods and a sustained reliability. This claim is advanced especially on behalf of branded goods. 'If a thing is advertised again and again, it's bound to be good' is the burden of many paragraphs and announcements in the Press. In 1940, for instance, when advertising was first threatened with the drastic reductions which were later effected, the Advertising Association issued a number of posters with the double aim of urging manufacturers to keep on advertising (because 'Brand goodwill is a capital asset of almost unlimited value: difficult to build: only too easy to lose') and persuading the public that there is 'Safety in a Name. You can rely upon advertised goods which bear the manufacturer's name or trade mark. His reputation is at stake and cannot be risked by varying the quality of his products.' The article on Advertising in the *Encyclopædia Britannica* (14th ed.) also argues that advertising standardises products and their quality; the use of brand names ensures a certain recognised standard of quality which the public has been educated to receive. And Miss Dorothy Sayers explains that the advertiser's

> reputation is in the long run his livelihood. An anonymous purveyor may sand his sugar or put paper in the soles of the shoes he sells; but if the advertiser of branded goods does so, then every time his distinctive name-block appears in print the disillusioned public will grit its teeth and get cold feet. His victims will talk; his bad name will be bandied about (16).

These claims on behalf of the part that advertising plays in the economic life of the country are extensive. If we accept them we shall have to agree that advertising is the motive power of industry, that 'if advertising ceased ... supply would swamp demand and economic and social chaos would be the outcome' (17). Given fairly normal conditions, says the writer just quoted, depressions are impossible if you advertise. 'Where advertising is employed to stimulate public demand the channels of distribution remain freer and more open' (18). In short, it is the view of many advertising experts, in their own words, that commercial prosperity depends on confidence; and that this can be attained if manufacturers are men of vision, sincerity and inspiration, and show their faith in the future by employing the services of counsellors in marketing.

This is in brief the case for advertising on economic grounds; and before we discuss it I would like to cite a few examples of how advertisement campaigns have produced results, without at the moment making any deductions from these successes. First, a frivolous instance: the case of the California Ranching Co., which proposed to start a cat and rat ranch, feeding the rats to the cats, the cats to the rats, and selling the skins at a daily profit of $10,000. Actually the company merely figured in a window advertisement of the Guardian Savings and Trust Company of Cleveland, warning savers to beware of buying worthless securities: 'It is a foolish fake, of course, but no more foolish than very many wild-cat schemes being promoted to-day. . . . Don't hand your money over to any unknown glib-tongued salesman.' Immense crowds gathered in front of the window, and applications, by post and in person, for the shares were so numerous that the advertisement had to be withdrawn (19).

To exemplify the success of advertising in creating demand for new products, the case of Curly Top ('the natural hair-curling preparation for babies') is cited first. Towards the end of 1935 the manufacture of Curly Top began in the rooms of a house in Bury, Lancs.; the work of mixing and bottling was done by a man and a boy. Advertising on an ascending scale was employed and three years later the Vosemar Co. needed a factory of 10,000 square feet to handle Curly Top (13). Other blessings which advertising has brought to humanity—frequently cited by experts—are Amami shampoos and Milton disinfectant, which increased its turnover fifty times in five years by advertising (20).

It may be suggested at this point that only an exceptionally credulous section of society can be knocked off its balance by the wind of advertising, but there is no evidence for that. One of the most interesting things about 'high-brow', humorous, or ironical (at its own expense) advertising is the way in which it succeeds in pleasing the educated public, and even in gaining respectful references in the columns of respectable weeklies, such as the *Spectator*. The way in which a sophisticated person falls a victim to advertising is indicated by this stock response: 'Of course most adverts are perfectly dreadful, but I do think the latest Austin Reeds are rather amusing.' This is exactly how the advertiser wishes his prospect to respond. It is also surprising to find that doctors—members of a profession which one might have thought proof against patent medicine advertisements—can be influenced by pressure of publicity just as much as any other section of the community. This is proved by 'the steady increase in the amount of drugs prescribed under proprietary names' (8).

There are plenty of examples of advertising successes in developing the sale of existing products, especially when a brand name can be used to defeat competition. '232' flannel trousers, for instance, were put on the market in 1922 and sold 3,000 pairs after a year without advertising. In 1923 £800 was spent in the *Daily Mail*. Sales rose to 60,000 pairs and by 1930 over half a million had been sold (21). More spectacular was the way in which we in England were made to buy a brand of raisins because the American Raisin Growers' Association had to get rid of a surplus. In the words of Stanley Q. Grady:

With the bumper crop coming on, the farmers decided to extend their market, and Europe seemed the most logical place to enter. A year ago last February, therefore, I went to England to start the initial campaign there. I spent two months organising an advertising campaign and selling force. The British didn't want our Sun Maid Raisins. For eighty years certain interests there had controlled the dried fruit market and had succeeded in keeping it a bulk market. As a bulk market, without an established brand, the dealers could absolutely control it. They could buy in South Africa, Australia, or anywhere they could purchase to the best advantage. With the advent of

B

an established brand, that power would pass, so they didn't intend to have Sun Maid Raisins go on the market.

But the American farmers had to have that market; England had to take part of that surplus crop if it was to be merchandised, so the British boycott was answered by the biggest food campaign London has ever had. The farmers spent two hundred and fifty thousand dollars in sixteen weeks in London alone. Front pages in all London papers were used, together with the most complete poster-showing possible in London. Hoardings, buses, the underground subways, even the freight wagons, were covered with Sun Maid Raisin posters. At the end of three weeks we had seven thousand retail accounts. Then the jobbers had to come in, and that little five-cent package blazed the trail. The big packages followed, and twenty thousand tons were sold in Great Britain in the past year (22).

This account and its context, which describes how the British and American consumers were sampled at their own expense, may be commended to newspaper proprietors interested in the Empire.

Co-operative advertising campaigns, too, have had some successes. The collective advertising of beer probably had something to do with the rise in consumption from 18,000,000 barrels in 1932-3 to 24,250,000 barrels in 1937-8 (13), though this is not so striking a result as that of the first year's large-scale advertising for Guinness, which produced an extra £900,000 for Revenue. The first six years of the importers' 'Eat more Fruit' campaign (23) increased fruit imports by 78%, and in a rather different way the expenditure by the railways of some hundreds of thousands of pounds in 1938 on advertising their need for a 'square deal' produced the required legislation (24).

It is time now to consider the case made out for advertising on economic grounds. In discussing the claim first stated—that advertising cheapens goods—we may make a rough division between basic products and services, serving essential needs, on the one hand, and on the other consumption goods and services, without which life would be possible. So far as items in the first class are concerned—food, clothing, and shelter—it is not easy to see how advertising lowers their prices. The consumer will feed and clothe and house himself as well as he can afford, and if advertising stopped entirely (as we can see from its war-time reduction) we should be no worse off. It does seem at first sight that the advertising of staples must increase their price; the consumer pays for the producer's expenditure on competing with other firms. It is difficult to find detailed evidence, and the advertisers will not often admit what the Director of Sales of the American Dairymen's League let out. After describing how his organisation put across the sale of a new brand of evaporated milk, he explains:

> Although the campaign will cost the League for the year approximately a quarter of a million dollars in the Metropolitan area, it is more than offset by the increased price and additional outlets they are getting for their commodity. For, at the opening of the campaign, the League advanced their price to the full price of the best known brands, such as . . . Carnation, and what is more they are getting it (22).

The aim of much advertising is in fact to sell products at prices above those of competing products—especially those which are less well known. Examples will be given later, but it is worth mentioning as a typical case the difference in price between acetylsalicylic acid tablets ('aspirin') of advertised and unadvertised makes; the former cost up to six times as much as the latter. Where advertising can change the consumer's valuation of a product, the price is likely to go up. The consumer is buying words, purchasing reputation.

In theory, and perhaps sometimes in practice, if competition between advertisers ends in the disappearance of inferior goods, the survivors can mass-produce on a large scale at a constant rate and offer a cheaper and better product.

I am not aware of any examples precisely of this process, but it is probably true that the multiple clothing firms exemplify low retail charges made possible by big sales promoted by advertising; and it was specifically claimed that the (pre-war) reduction in the price of the ten h.p. Vauxhall represented 'the passing on to the consumer of economies in the cost of production made possible by the increasing popularity of the car'. But if an advertiser succeeds in establishing a monopoly, prices are almost bound to rise—in the shape it may be of smaller packages or poorer quality. It is axiomatic that monopolies tend to restrict output or charge high prices, or both.

But there is no reason why we should not have the benefits of mass-production without advertising. If a manufacturer gets increased sales without advertising he can reduce his prices and yet make the same total profit. Though the branded makes are well advertised, bicycles as a whole used to be cheap because they were made in quantities in response to a genuine demand for a useful machine. And in the case of many marginal necessities we could—and do at Woolworths and Marks & Spencers—enjoy the fruits of mass-production without sales-promotion; low factory costs are not cancelled out by high distribution costs. This has happened with certain products (such as beer and petrol); they carry large advertising appropriations from which no advantage accrues to the consumer, because savings in production are offset by expenditure on space in the Press and on hoardings, or on salesmen and canvassers. Another way in which the savings of mass-producing are nullified by costly distribution is this: entrepreneurs are sometimes too optimistic, assume an almost unlimited market, sink more money in plant than is justified by the potential demand, and eventually have to hand on to the retail buyer the cost of working up sales to dispose of the output, and maintain a factory larger than is needed. There are cases known where this has happened (one of an expensive factory being dumped in a beautiful part of Surrey to satisfy a demand which not even advertising could create), but the process is more typical of the U.S.A. Robert Lynd notes that:

> In a rough sense plant expansion follows consumer demand; actually, however, guided by guess and plans for capturing the volume market, expansion tends to leap ahead of actual demand; and it outlasts demand. Once built, on the basis of whatever expectations, expanded plant facilities increase overhead and become compelling stimuli to sales pressure on the consumer (25).

Mention should be made here of an attractive argument in favour of advertising, i.e. that by cutting out the wholesale distributor and shortening the route between producer and consumer, it allows a lower retail price to be charged. Storage and transport costs are lowered, and goods are fresher when sold. But I have not come across an example of a product of which the price had been lower by advertising in this way. It is true that there are instances (some makes of radio set) of sales being increased without cost to the consumer; here the retailer usually has to accept a lower discount, which in theory is compensated by increased business. This is an exception to the generalisation that the consumer pays for advertising.

We come next to the assertion that advertising justifies itself by the information it gives; and memories of pre-war hoardings and a glance at a newspaper will show that but a very small proportion of displayed advertisements provide information about new products. The aim of the rest is to increase the sales of an established line or to maintain its position against competition; and of these too a very small number offer any information about the product they advertise. Especially when a number of cigarette-brands are competing, there is simply nothing to be said about one that is not equally true of another. So the aim of many advertisements is positively not to give any information, but to sell illusion (cf. p. 128). When there are many brands of a commodity of the same quality and price the easiest method is to recommend them on irrelevant grounds rather than on a basis of reason.

Advertising does sometimes perform the function of giving information, as in the case of the monthly lists of new books compiled by the wholesalers, and in the advertisement pages of technical journals addressed to experts. But even where it does give information, it is often an unduly expensive and haphazard channel for matter which could be better diffused by other methods; and the facts may be so selected and presented as to give a quite false impression. Examples will be cited when truth in advertising is discussed, but before leaving this aspect I would like to quote the view of a responsible critic:

> The major part of *informative* advertising is, and always has been, a campaign of exaggeration, half-truths, intended ambiguities, direct lies, and general deception. Amongst all the hundreds of thousands of persons engaged in the business, it may be said about most of them on the informative side of it that their chief function is to deceive buyers as to the real merits and demerits of the commodity being sold (26).

One of the benefits most insistently claimed for advertising is the raising of the standard of living. It is true that advertising has been the means (but not necessarily the source) whereby fresh activities, labour-saving devices and luxuries have been introduced to people who would not otherwise have felt the need of them. It is true that advertising has made more people want more things. It has 'created wants', succeeded in diverting expenditure from one channel to another; but whether this is an advantage to society or to the individual depends on the nature of the new needs. A great deal of ingenuity and energy has been spent in adding to the wants of the fifth century Athenian or the eighteenth century Englishman, but they would have been better employed in devising a distributive machine which would allow the basic needs of all members of society to be satisfied.

Advertising may have brought a higher standard of material living to those who can afford it, but it cannot be said to have increased the number of these people. Advertising does not augment the national wealth; it merely modifies the distribution of national expenditure. It may mean that wages go to the dogs rather than to books and education, to smoking rather than savings and insurance, to the pools[1] rather than to good food and creative leisure. (I am aware that some economists consider that too much money goes on saving and insurance, slowing up the circulation of money; if they are right, advertising can be made to serve the interests of society. But it ought to be socially controlled.) On ethical and cultural grounds too the higher standard has come in for a good deal of censure from sociologists and others. (This will be discussed in Chapter III.) They point out that for all our higher standard we are not properly housed, healthier or more contented. Any genuine raising of the standard that may have occurred must, they say, be attributed not to advertising but to inventions, improved manufacturing methods, wider knowledge of hygiene and increased purchasing power.

Before I leave this topic it should be added that an advantage of some advertising is that it brings the producer into closer contact with the real needs of the consumer and causes him to standardise quality at a higher level (21).

Mr. Taylor also points out one of the disadvantages of the branded goods system. The consumer becomes conditioned

---

[1] At the time of Mr. Rowntree's investigations in York (27), 48,000 pools circulars were posted to houses in that city every week. 'There is no doubt', he says, 'that among a vast number of people, football pools have become an obsession, and actually constitute the chief interest of their lives.'

to asking for products by their advertised rather than their generic names; this, of course, is the aim of much advertising —'Don't buy paint, buy Luc'—or whatever it may be. Thus the retailer tends 'merely to hand over goods and receive money instead of using his expert knowledge in advising the consumer'. It may be replied that the retailer needs to be little more than a slot machine because branded goods are necessarily better than unbranded, according to the usual assertion that the brand calls attention to faults as easily as it wins recognition for merits. There are two flaws in the argument: it omits the fact that the producer of unbranded goods must also maintain a standard of quality, because he sells through the wholesalers and retailers who are in a better position to judge—much more so than the inexpert consumer. This suggests the second fallacy: that the consumer is competent to judge for himself. He rarely is, despite all the flattery of advertising; there are very few fields where he has the necessary technical knowledge to be capable of deciding for himself. And even if he has the capacity, it is surprising how advertising can nullify it. In such matters as the taste of food, the flavour of a cigarette, the scent of a soap, the public may make its own decisions—though even here the choice may be influenced by advertising; but that, anyway, does not matter much. When it comes to evaluating the quality of soap, food, medicine, cars, household goods, the consumer is at sea, though he rarely knows it. Because 'an advertiser does not have to ensure that his goods are of high quality; he has to ensure that the consumer *thinks* that the quality is high— which may be a very different matter' (21).

It is not easy to secure impartial information on the merits of advertised and unadvertised goods. A writer in the *New Statesman* (6 December 1941) records that he made analyses of oil products which were published in a paper:

> Their analyses indicated that certain little-known products were of approximately the same quality as some of the very

heavily advertised brands which sold at higher prices. This immediately brought complaints from advertisers, and the publication of these analyses had to cease.

The consumer's ignorance is much exploited by the advertisements for many foods and proprietary medicines. A make of meat cube of which a sample was said to contain 65% salt in 1920 is still advertised and selling, though the proportion of salt was much less in a sample analysed for me in 1940. The case of ** (46) shows what can be done for a patent medicine by advertising; there is no reason to suppose that in its fraudulent claims and worthless ingredients it was an isolated case. As the American, E. A. Filene, wrote:

Poor values can be sold by large persistent advertising. It is simply a question of psychology—the hammering into people's minds of a certain idea until finally they accept it. If the sacrifice to accept it is not so big as to make a constant reinvestigation necessary . . . they will submit to the suggestion that a certain thing at a certain price is the best on the market (21).

So far is the consumer unable to judge the merits of two brands of the same product that advertising sometimes persuades him to buy goods of inferior merit. Branded varieties of cheese and raisins, for example, are often inferior to the unbranded. The packed and labelled versions of cheese save the retailer trouble and allow it to be kept longer, but they are often adulterated and of poor flavour. Reduction in the quality or quantity (in a pack) of branded goods may often be caused by increased expenditure on advertising or by a price reduction as a selling point.

It is also said that branding eliminates complaints, and this is true in so far as the powerful suggestion and reiteration of advertising makes for a more complaisant customer. The writer's experience is that it enables the retailer to evade the responsibility for a faulty or dangerous product. If you buy loose unbranded soap powder with an excess of free alkali causing soda dermatitis with complications causing some days in a hospital, there is a chance of discussing the matter with the retailer so that he will warn others. But if, as the writer's wife did, you suffer the results described from using a branded soap powder, heavily advertised as being safe for the hands, you will find that a large firm which has bought impunity with advertising neglects to answer a statement of the facts. And anyone who cares to litigate will find that it is almost impossible to prove in law that a certain trouble was caused by an advertised product, and that a wealthy firm is almost impregnable against a claim backed only by facts. It so happened about the same time that proceedings were reported in the Press against the maker of an advertised washing powder on the ground that it had caused similar trouble, but failed.

Heavily advertised brand names are often used to impose a tax on homogeneous and standard substances, capitalising consumer ignorance, and making it difficult to buy unbranded varieties of the goods required. An advertising agent writes:

> A well-known soap flake with a branded name is advertised to the extent of £150,000 a year. The profits are reputed to be £500,000 a year. There are two non-advertised soap flakes the prices of which are considerably less; one is less by half. The chemical composition of all three articles is exactly the same (28).

Trichlorethylene (before the present war) sold in bulk at 4s. 9d. a gallon; under proprietary names it is sold bottled as a stain remover at from four to eight times the price. There is a similar difference between the price of cream of tartar or sodium phosphate, sold loose at a chemist's (2d. per ounce), and the price of the same substances when bottled and advertised as fruit or liver salts.

Some breakfast foods provide other examples. Advertised wheat flakes sell at 1s. 3d. a pound. Before the war the wholesale price of wheat was 5s. 3d. a hundred pounds or between ½d. and ¾d. a pound. The price of the finished product is therefore twenty-three times that of the raw material, though it is impossible to say how this is divided between manufacturing, packing, distributing and advertising costs. This ratio of 1 : 20 holds good for most advertised breakfast cereals. Advertising must contribute largely to the cost of many other products. An anonymous fountain pen sold at 3s. 6d. may give service as good as another well-known make priced at from 7s. 6d. to £2 2s., for the advertising of which in one month sixteen half-pages in national newspapers and periodicals, and thirty-two half-pages in provincial papers were purchased, in addition to window displays.

In discussions about branded goods one often finds it suggested that a trade name brings better packaging; and this is important in the case of foodstuffs which can be sold more cleanly and conveniently in packets. But there is no reason at all why we should not have packaging, where desirable, without the addition of a brand name. The difference, for example, in price between packed and loose sugar used to be negligible; and the packets were not made on elaborate lines for advertising purposes. They frequently are, in the case of other goods; and what we pay for them was suggested by a 'Modern Packaging' supplement to the *Daily Telegraph*. It gave £16,000,000 as the value of paper containers produced in a year; £3,290,000 for metal containers; £5,222,000 for glass containers; and over £11,000,000 for other types. Before the present war, the production value of industries associated with packaging was not less than £60,000,000 a year.

In general, the advertising of branded goods represents an impost used in an attempt to build and maintain a monopoly reputation. Where this does not succeed, we get competition between home manufacturers and distributors, the cost of which, from the consumer's point of view, is nine-tenths wasted. If a monopoly or near-monopoly is established, we are likely to find advertising used to maintain sales at a high price, while the quality may drop to the minimum it is possible to sell. In short:

> Advertising and selling devices generally are the methods which can be used to work upon such factors in the market as ignorance or inertia or shortsightedness in space or time, and from these raw materials to create more spectacular attachments and preferences for the products of a particular firm. Of this the modern vogue of branded goods and proprietary articles is a special case; while the increasing rôle played in the modern world by the distributive apparatus and by distributive costs is its inevitable product (29).

The use of brand names is likely to develop, if the tendencies evident before 1939 continue after the war. There are already many advertisements which try to make us ask for a name instead of a product. The attachment of a brand and an illusory value to simple substances has reached its height in the cosmetic and patent medicine fields, and food is now being exploited—in America Idaho potatoes are sometimes wrapped up separately like oranges, with a brand. 'The trade-name is a priceless ingredient for which we are willing to pay a fancy price. In luxury goods like cosmetics, the trade-name is all-important, because it provides the only element of exclusiveness, which is necessary to satisfaction. In necessities, the creation of illusory values goes on just as rapidly . . .' (*Economic Behaviour*, by Willard E. Atkins and others). A reliance on brands appears to have spread to an unexpected class of consumers; when the late *Week-end Review* submitted a questionnaire on advertising to its readers, 48% of the replies stated that in buying goods they relied chiefly on the producer's brand, 19% relied on confidence in the distributor, and 33% claimed to exercise personal judgment. An exhibit at an Advertising and Marketing exhibition suggests to a writer in the *Observer* the potentialities of branding and packaging:

Here women will find their dream shop, Packeteria, the stores of 1950, whose stock will include water sold in cardboard boxes, so that no more will a picnic fail dismally at the otherwise perfect spot because fresh drinking water is not to be had. The consumer will help himself in this perfect shop, and what she buys will be taken to the door for her on a miniature railway. Among ingenious packages of all kinds there is a new container for rice, which on one side has a window graduated in ounces. . . .

There is a good deal of scepticism about advertising; but it is common to find that critics who condemn it as misleading, unscrupulous and generally anti-social reluctantly admit that it is still essential to the working of the present economic system. The fact that the Press reports only the observations of those who favour advertising has something to do with the prevalence of this opinion. Actually the field in which advertising is useful is comparatively small; it is employed by a minority of consumption industries, and by some of them only because competition compels it. The basic industries—iron, coal, rubber—rarely employ advertising because the demand is inelastic, and because they are selling to consumers who know what they are buying, though for years advertising agents have been urging the heavy industries to alter their selling methods; and since the war advertising has spread to all sorts of heavy and light engineering firms. Some concerns and some banks advertise because by so doing they can put the money down as expenses and save a good deal of income tax. This merits the attention of the Chancellor of the Exchequer.

The building trade is an example of a socially useful industry; its products are necessary and a high proportion of the cost goes in wages. It has only a limited use for advertising. Much of the publicity connected with it—in the pages for instance of the *Architectural Review*—exemplify desirable advertising; these pages carry announcements of building materials and accessories, but their intention and method are very different from those of poster and displayed advertising. The vendor of building materials wishes to inform the architects and contractors, equipped with technical knowledge, that his products are available. The methods accord. There is none of the over-emphasis, persuasion or insinuation seen in displayed advertisements—wherein the vendor is approaching a consumer who is not competent to test the actual quality of the goods against the claims made for them. So far as the finished house is concerned advertising is much used, and some of it is strictly informative. But it is mainly applied to dwellings for the middle class, which is comparatively well-off for houses. It is the lowest wage-earner who needs houses, and the demand makes advertising superfluous. The margin of profit here does not in any case allow much for publicity; and no amount of this could make the lower wage-earner take on a house beyond his means. Advertising cannot make up for a deficiency of purchasing power.

To return to the consumption goods. The volume of their sales depends on national prosperity, which is but slightly affected by advertising; all the advertisers can do is to compete for a share of the nation's purchasing power—or that part of it which is not spent on the basic needs. Three-fifths of the retail turnover in this country carries less than one-tenth of what is spent on advertising, according to Mr. S. C. Leslie, Publicity Manager of the Gas Light and Coke Company (30). What would happen if we stopped spending the remaining nine-tenths? The country would lose little; the products for which there is a genuine demand would continue to sell—on their merits, perhaps. National prosperity does not depend on the goods recommended on the hoardings and in displayed advertising. Some of the products which account for the two-fifths of the retail turnover that spends so much on publicity might suffer; there would be unemployment in some trades for a time, but this might be fully compensated by freer spending in other channels where distributive costs represent a smaller, and wage costs a higher proportion of the retail price.

Any criticism of advertising implies criticism of the economy in which it plays a part; and the aim here is not to make advertising a scapegoat, but to isolate it for inspection. Actually there is no strong argument to show that it is essential even to the existing distributive machine—economists of differing schools seem to agree in ignoring it—and there is a good deal of evidence the other way. In the present system its useful functions are limited. Professor Pigou, discussing how Industrial Fluctuations (in the book of that title) can be avoided, concludes that as regards 'luxury and semi-luxury consumption goods, for which the demand is fairly elastic, a good deal might be done in this way (greater expenditure on advertising and salesmanship) to stabilise production at no great cost to the producers. But for those important instrumental goods, the demand, from a short-period point of view, is likely to be highly inelastic; and this means that sales could not be pushed much in bad times except at the cost of a very large fall in prices, and, therefore, of a very heavy loss to the manufacturers.'

Advertising, therefore, may be useful in stimulating consumption when necessary, but unfortunately there is no authority to decide when this is necessary. Like all stimulants, it is injurious at the wrong time and in the wrong quantity. It can, for example, help to promote instalment buying, which is a rather clumsy and dangerous attempt to provide consumers with credit in a time of depression—a want which Mr. J. E. Meade would satisfy by creating new money and giving it to consumers to spend on consumption goods. 'But if the money subsequently required to meet instalments is found by abstaining from other forms of consumption, there is ultimately no gain in aggregate consuming power; all that happens is that demand is diverted from little marginal luxuries—shoes, cigarettes, beer and cinemas—or even from food, to more or less durable household furniture and gadgets' (9). And it is generally agreed that vast transactions on the instalment plan in the U.S.A. disorganised industry and contributed to at least one slump by over-stimulating production and mortgaging future purchasing power. Advertising tends to be cut down in a slump and enlarged in a boom. Thus it accentuates the movements of the trade cycle by discouraging consumption and employment when business is bad, and vice-versa. As the *Economist* has pointed out, it should be managed in just the opposite way.

Advertising may not be a sufficiently important factor for the professional economist to consider; or the neglect of it may be due to the fact that it has introduced the working of a new element into the working of supply and demand, to deal with which the technique of economists is at present inadequate. The classical interplay of demand and supply does not fit the facts of a situation in which a distributive machine of great cost lies between producer and consumer, where the producer tries hard to control his market instead of merely supplying an existent demand, and where as a result consumption is a more complex affair and the producer more potent than before—if he succeeds in establishing a monopoly or near-monopoly. The calculations of economists are upset, for instance, by the phenomenon—noted in the U.S.A. as being due to advertising—of rising wholesale prices on a market in which labour and raw material costs are declining. The theories of the classical economist do not apply to present conditions, because

'The forces of competition' which in the classical theory performed a useful and social function as the instrument by which social interest dominated individual interest, cheapening products and promoting innovation, to-day appear as a costly apparatus for resisting the operation of 'the unseen hand' of social interest and for the manufacture of restrictive monopoly rights (29).

III. Who pays?

In discussing the question 'Whom does it pay to advertise?' we considered and rejected the claim that it benefits
society. It has now to be shown that on certain classes of
goods it is the consumer that pays heavily for advertising,
and—by examining the slogan 'Truth in Advertising'—
that the consumer pays in other ways besides being over-
charged.

The greatest waste through advertising occurs when it is
used as a weapon of competition. Once a producer in a particular line starts advertising, the others must follow, and
eventually the *status quo ante* is reached, at the consumer's
expense. An example of this was the introduction by the
Daily Herald of house-to-house canvassing for newspaper
readers; this cost individual papers thousands of pounds a
year, and probably seven figures for Fleet Street as a whole,
according to the PEP *Report on the Press.* New permanent
readers secured by this method cost up to £2 a head, and
then the permanency was dubious. Generally speaking, an
entrepreneur cannot break into a market without a costly
publicity campaign, and once in he has to maintain his
position by unremitting advertising. Inter-industrial advertising, of the type which invites us to go by rail rather than by
road, to buy correspondence courses instead of cigarettes, is
again a tax on the consumer—and a socially undesirable one
if it leads, say, to expenditure on cars instead of education, on
having a good time rather than on insurance.

It is time now to give a few concrete examples of the way
in which advertising increases costs, by being utilised as a
competitive weapon. It has come about that the expense of
marketing and advertising certain goods is almost equal to
the cost of producing them. The Secretary Treasurer of the
Associated Advertising Clubs of the world says (22) that in
America:

c

but ten to seventeen cents of the consumer's dollar, on a rough average, represents the cost of manufacture . . . the cost of production and manufacture together is less than the total cost of selling, transportation, and delivery. In plain words, it costs more to sell goods than it does to produce them.

And that this is not the exaggeration of an enthusiast is shown by the increase in the U.S.A. of the ratio of workers engaged in distribution to those engaged in production; it has increased from 20 : 80 in 1850 to 50 : 50 at present.

The proportion of the retail price that goes on publicity is least in the case of necessaries. 'Meat, milk, butter, fruit, vegetables, bread, sugar, tea, fuel, light, many sorts of clothing—this list in the aggregate probably has less than a fifth of a penny spent on its advertising for every pound of sales.' Mr. Leslie's estimate was for 1933, and owing to the development of collective advertising (of milk, fruit, bread, tea, light) since then it is now probably on the low side. On the other hand, when we come to luxury and semi-luxury goods, the advertising bill is high. In the case of cars, for instance, Mr. J. N. Leonard considers that advertising, especially in the higher price ranges, has made the new car public pay for more quality and performance than it needs, and that this, together with advertising and distribution, is holding up the price of cars; otherwise a cheap utility car could be sold for £40 (31). Normally such facts are kept from the motorist, but the war-time need for durability is bringing the truth home, and it is being even recognised in the motoring papers, which are normally very kind to advertised products. The *Autocar* (2 January 1942) submits that too much has been heard of 'performance' when applied to the normal car for the family man; the same editorial suggests that there has been a tendency for manufacturers to offer too much in relation to cost of car, and that such a policy may result in disappointment for the buyer. There is a similar impost upon the car's fuel; the cost of refining petrol is a bare ½d. more than that of refining Diesel oil, but at retail, petrol costs 5d. more. This is accounted for partly by an excessive number of petrol pumps, and partly by distributive and advertising costs. In peace time it was possible to buy lubricating oil of the same specification as that of advertised brands at half the price; not only did the oil companies spend lavishly on publicity but also they used to give thousands of gallons of oil away to car manufacturers in return for an official recommendation.

Competitive advertising of a particularly senseless kind was indulged in by cigarette firms before the war. It is said that cigarettes which in peace-time sold at ten for 6d. could have been priced at ten for 4½d., but for huge selling costs (28). Constituent companies of the same combine used to carry on sham fights against one another, and even if this is considered necessary to keep sales up, it is waste from the consumer's point of view—for the quality of most cheap cigarettes is the same, the main difference being in the packing and brand name. Mr. F. W. Taylor quotes the chairman of a tobacco firm: 'During the past eighteen months there have been cases where between £100,000 and £300,000 has been spent in an attempt to create a demand for a single brand of cigarettes without any impression having been made on sales' (21). This went in coupon schemes and gifts of boots (one and a quarter million pairs by one firm) in addition to normal advertisements.

Necessities also are weighted with advertising costs. Even milk requires a large margin of profit, according to a government Committee of Investigation, because of excessive distributing costs which included money wasted on canvassing; and the advertising of patent foods necessitated a counter campaign by the Milk Marketing Board. The additional refining (a talking point) and packaging (for branding) of salt have increased the price of salt tenfold. Books are an example of advertising being introduced as a competitive weapon by one firm and then employed by others, with no gain to the publishing trade in the end. Mr. Stanley Unwin has shown (32) that large book sales are never the result of advertising alone, that excessive advertising will not produce results commensurate with the expenditure, and that indiscriminate advertising is foolish and wasteful. The advertising of toilet articles, like that of patent medicines, may account for anything up to a quarter of the retail price. A memorandum of the Department of Health for Scotland noted that

> Unnecessarily high cost (in prescriptions) can also be caused by the use of certain proprietary medicines which, in spite of the quasi-scientific claims made for them, can be replaced by equally pure, effective and much less costly medicaments.

Examples were given:

> Prescribe Paraff. Moll. Flav. at 1d. per ounce and not Vaseline at 2d. per ounce; prescribe Calcium Sodium Lactate Tablets 50 at 1s. 6½d. and not Kalzana Tablets 50 at 3s. 8½d. (33).

Even in the case of pharmaceutical products excellent in themselves large sums are spent on promoting their sale to doctors by free samples, hospitality, diaries, journals, and so on.

The following examples show how costly is the building up of 'good-will' by publicity. When in 1935 Macleans, Ltd., acquired the business of A.C.M. Ltd. the purchase price was £1,400,000 of which good-will and trade-marks accounted for £1,163,557. On this the *Observer* commented:

> This is a large sum and will no doubt be taken into consideration by investors. It should be pointed out, however, that it is not unusual in companies manufacturing proprietary articles to have a large goodwill item. Their earning capacity is dependent on continuous and widespread advertising, the capital invested in which is really the equivalent of capital invested by other concerns in more tangible assets. How much the

Maclean Company has spent in creating this goodwill it is impossible to say, for the prospectus is silent upon the point (9).

It should be added in parenthesis that Beecham's Pills in 1938 acquired the whole of the Ordinary capital of Macleans and nearly the whole of the Ordinary capital of Eno Proprietaries; and that the chairman of Beecham's Pills, Ltd., was able to announce in 1941 that their trading profits had for the ninth successive year shown an increase, to £1,085,893. In 1938 the same firm presented a block of research laboratories to the Royal Northern Hospital, Holloway. This gift (heralded by full page advertisements in the Press) is itself a form of advertising, but it is at least one in which society gets back something of what it has paid for advertising. However, it would be better to have research laboratories provided in a directer way than by this somewhat roundabout method; and it is desirable that all laboratories should be quite free, as the Royal Northern is free, from any suspicion of commercial pressure when it comes to publishing analyses of, say, proprietary medicines.

One more piece of evidence about the advertising of proprietaries should be added. When Kruschen profits fell in 1937 from £456,678 to £234,401 the *Economist* for May 22 commented:

> Proprietary medicine finance is full of incalculables. Investors have no knowledge of the value of their chief asset—goodwill—until the results are published. The holding company's capitalisation is based on a purchase of profits rather than fixed assets, and the profits record, in turn, is dependent upon advertising expenditure. The latter item forms the clue both to current profits (being far and away the greatest element of cost) and to their future maintenance . . . shareholders deserve the fullest information on this particular aspect of the company's finance, since 1930. The company has passed beyond the 'aggressive' stage in its market; is it possible that it is now paying the cost in reduced profits?

For all this expenditure on advertising it is the consumer who pays directly. There are also less obvious forms of waste to be considered. Even from the advertiser's point of view there is waste when unsuitable methods or channels are used. In some cases this may be the fault of the advertising agencies. The newspapers pay them by commission on the amount of space they buy for their clients in the Press: so the natural tendency is for the agency to advocate a Press campaign for promoting a product, for which mail advertising might be much more effective and economical. Anyhow advertising is a very uncertain method; in one case £41 spent in one paper was as effective as £57 in another and £1,108 in another (21). Certain goods and services are quite unadapted to selling by advertising at all.

Even the advertising experts admit that from their point of view much expenditure is wasteful—60% according to Sir William Crawford. The sheepish way in which some advertisers imitate each other's methods exemplifies this. The strip cartoon has been exploited *ad nauseam*, and must fail to work upon many readers. The writer has glanced through a whole clip of cartoons advertising a certain product, and ended by falling a victim to suggestion, thinking how nice a warm cup of drink O would be—to find as he was putting them away that it was drink H that was being recommended. In one issue of a daily, motor tyres, breakfast food and soap were being pushed by three or four illustrated testimonials, each from Average Men and Women, all laid out in the same way. The effect was a blur, the one cancelling out the other. Not only the advertisers, but also the producers imitate each other. Products which sold well enough before they were advertised, have to be modified 'in some way quite irrelevant to (their) main qualifications for satisfying a real need. In other words, a "selling point" has to be thought of, some trivial embellishment that carries the product in to popular favour along some well-worn channel of high-pressure salesmanship; and further waste thereby occurs' (26).

This brings us to a third way in which advertising and the processes in which it is instrumental entail a waste of energy and material—the high rate of obsolescence and rapid style changes which many technical writers have lamented. It is the advertiser's business to keep the turnover moving, and this is effected more easily if goods can be made to wear out quickly, or if the consumer can be persuaded or shamed into thinking that they need frequent replacement. Stuart Chase (34) points out that by doubling the life of cars, furniture, socks and so on, the quantity of goods for distribution theoretically doubles without much increase in cost. But as it is, it is logical and inevitable that in an economic system dominated by vendibility, consumer goods are in many cases made under the compulsion of rapid replacement; low quality goods are deliberately manufactured to wear out quickly. And this, of course, involves a waste of labour, material and machine efficiency.

The annual model racket is a well-known illustration. New editions of cars, for instance, are produced every year; in many cases the difference between the new and the old model is trifling and confined to talking points only. If important changes really were made every year in a mass-produced car, it would be evidence of bad designing. It would probably be wasteful to force up any further the exchange rate of typewriters and sewing-machines; there have been few significant changes in design for thirty years, and some makes of these machines will actually last that time. Dress is another example of calculated obsolescence, especially in U.S.A., where there is a bigger population, and manufacturers to mass-produce for it. In his *Report on America* Robert Waithman notes that the style industry is as big as the steel industry, and depends on the will of women to dress attractively not being allowed to flag for a moment. 'It is kept going by a broadside of advertising which in the last ten years has risen to such a crescendo that women have no chance of pausing, no time for doubting. . . . The thing is a steam roller, flattening resistance, deadening all uncertainty, making it clear in every way that this is the purpose of life.' The salesman's demand for style changes means that emphasis is laid all the time on appearance and superficial details; 'good looks' are being made a selling point even in the marketing of cameras, and the inane taste for 'stream-lining' developed by advertising has reached numerous products—kitchen cabinets for example—where it has not the slightest relevance; I have seen the wheels of a weighing machine enclosed in a stream-lined mudguard. If the annual model ramp is developed again we shall find that we are in sight of the goal foreseen by one observer (34), where the function of the buyer is to pay for the privilege of casually inspecting the article as it moves from factory to junk-heap.

The loss entailed by advertising may be borne in several ways; by reduced profits to the producers, by a lower discount for the retailer, by lower wages for the worker, by the extinction of competing firms, by society in higher prices, poorer quality, or in ways that will be described next.

Advertising involves a loss to society in the misdirection of energy and talent and in the misuse of time and material. Some aspects of this will be discussed in Chapter III, but some properly belong here. Lewis Mumford notes that

> In an effort to force a 'national' market, against the natural regional affiliations and standards, an enormous amount of energy has been thrown into sales organisations, into advertising, into fashion publicity, which might have been better used to raise the purchasing power of labor and to assist in a reorganisation on regional lines of the essential means of production. All these wastes are paid for, not merely in money, but in confusion of mind and social deterioration (35).

That quotation needs no explanation. I should now like to quote an advertisement for an agency, which appeared in a Supplement, *The Power of Advertising*, to the *Daily Mail*, 19 June, 1939. It was headed 'Written after Hours' and the point of it was that the copywriters and other employees of the agency, so far from stopping work at five, continue their labours into the night:

> Across the passage a man bends over his desk, writing. Cigarette stubs pyramid his ashtray. From his window as he glances in thought he can look down on Smith Square, four floors below, and see the church like an inverted footstool in the gathering dusk. It is after hours, but he works on. He will whip his copy into finished form before he leaves his desk. His inspiration is the Goodyear Tyre. . . . One of the layout men has just left his drawing board and is going down in the lift. Under his arm he carries a tissue pad. A new idea is stirring in his mind. It will be roughed out in pencil before morning comes. Weeks, may be months from now you will see it in print, a finished advertisement for Hoover.

The advertisement went on at some length to describe how hours after the office had closed and the workers had gone home, the copy-writers at their homes in the suburbs or in the West End or in sleepers racing northward were thinking out ideas for new campaigns. It told the reader how a few scribbled notes on the back of an old letter might strike the key-note for a new drive on behalf of a breakfast food, how in the interval at a theatre a new idea for selling soap might take shape, how a famous advertising came back from a fishing holiday.

This is an ad. written for admen and potential clients. That is why no pains are taken to disguise a kind of fervour hitherto deemed more appropriate to religion and the arts. To the ordinary reader it is a little odd that the inspiration of a man toiling far into the night at forming ideas and whipping them into words should be—Goodyear Tyres. The mood evoked is more fitted to that in which artists and musicians are supposed to work; but agonised months of creative gestation produce—a blurb for a vacuum cleaner.

If this advertisement had been directed to the general public, one's reaction would have been: 'cynical stuff, done with tongue in cheek, to impress an unthinking reader with all the romance and genius involved in writing ballyhoo.' But it is not cynical, entirely. The writer at least half believes what he is saying. Some copywriters I understand do take themselves seriously as artists, perhaps because they are trying to justify themselves in working at what they know really to be worthless. A few years ago there was actually published an anthology of advertising copy, called *Prose of Persuasion*, and I believe that a selection from Callisthenes was also published in book form.

However one regards this particular advertisement, one is led to reflect that talent goes into advertising channels which under different conditions might have produced minor poems or paintings or pieces of research. The present economic system deprives us of the work of potential writers and painters; it turns on creative talent at points where, and in a form in which it does more harm than good. The expenditure of all this energy on boosting consumption goods contributes to the ill-balance of a society without the knowledge of what it really wants or the will to get it. Sir William Crawford once said that an advertising man should be 'as impartial as a judge, as impassioned as a poet, and he should possess the eye of an artist, clarity of mind, logic and business acumen'. And Mr. Dennis Bradley foresees 'the time—and that in the immediate future—when into the vortex of commerce, because of the fundamental instinct to live, will be swept all our great writers' (22). The residue of truth in these boasts is that in a society where mechanical progress appears at times to run itself in a non-human impersonal manner, where one of the most operative standards of value is vendibility, human beings seem to be moulded in a mechanical pattern, existing as consumers or feeders of consumers. In it the writer's job is propaganda of one sort or another. Advertising is the voice of civilisation. If the main drive of civilisation is getting people to buy more and yet more things, the channels of communication and the skill of writers will be engaged mainly in urging the need for acquisition.

To return to the practical and unspeculative. The diversion of creative talent into advertising channels is a waste even of the business man's appropriation for publicity if it is spent 'to satisfy the romantic fervour of the advertising man dreaming away under his lamp, or to tickle the childlike vanity of the manufacturer who sees his product more beautiful than he ever thought it could be' (36). Because:

> The kind of work on goods that profits the consumer is not done with words, but with tools and instruments, and by the aid of calculations, reference books, and other dull, routine devices not at all likely to delight the mind that fashions un-realities into 'sales-thrusts', 'creative merchandising' and drug-store romance (37).

To conclude this section there follows an examination of the slogan 'Truth in Advertising'—which was I believe adopted at the Boston Convention of the Associated Advertising Clubs of the world in 1911, though it was in 1924 that it became widely current. The chairman of the National Vigilance Committee of the Associated Advertising Clubs of the World assures us that 'advertising must be wholly truthful . . . all selling is based upon the confidence of the buyer. . . . No sales policy is permanently beneficial that has its roots in deception' (22).

The amount of direct falsehood in advertising is probably small; but there are many other ways of telling lies than by literal untruths. Facts may be selected, each in itself verifi-able, in such a way that a totally misleading impression is given; in a road v. rail war, for example, one newspaper might support the railways and point out how faithfully they served the public in peace and war, the amount of coal they used, the employment they gave, the pensions they paid their workers and so on, at the same time reporting fully every lorry or coach smash and dilating on such topics as the long hours and poor pay of transport drivers. Another paper might take the part of road transport, stress the romance of a big industry built up by independent operators from small beginnings, and show how much in revenue the Road Fund licences contributed to the State; simultaneously it would give prominence to every railway accident, produce statistics about the short lives of firemen, the long hours and poor pay of porters and dining-car attendants.

Statistics, too, are the easiest things with which to tell lies, especially in the form of percentages, to a public that has a vague respect for science and no notion of scientific method. Many advertisements that make play with figures remind one of the argument against teetotalism: 'In a certain Indian regiment half the total abstainers died in a year', the explanation being, of course, that there were two, one of whom was mauled by a tiger. The graph-depicting advertisement is rarely on a higher level than this. Generalisations based on selected instances are used by advertisers, just as they are by opponents of vaccination. Advertisements, too, commonly operate by choosing a ground for discussion which is miles away from the pertinent point. The stupid examination candidate, fabled by every schoolmaster, who said 'Far be it from me to answer the question set—let me rather give you a list of the Kings of Israel and of Judah', failed to get by anyone; but nearly everyone is taken in by advertisers using exactly the same recipe. The cigarette advertisement which says 'Blasters are Best' and supports the assertion by the picture of a pretty girl or the testimony of an actress works that way. Such announcements have shifted far away from the arena where facts substantiate argument, and the shift is deliberate; advertisements do not want people to think, so they keep off the plane of reason. The use of exaggeration, innuendo and half truth, and diversion from facts and reason to realms of illusion and wishfulfilment are all forms of non-truth. 'If truth means accuracy of detail, no misrepresentation of relative values, no undue enticement of the individual, no misleading implications, then there is little truth in advertising.' (Vaughan, *Marketing and Advertising*.)

One gets the impression that advertising experts themselves have not much belief in the slogan 'Truth in Advertising', and do not like discussing it. The phrase is meant to produce a certain response, to develop 'Consumer-confidence', not to make a statement. The real aim of advertisers is shown in an American's injunctions on planning a campaign:

> People . . . buy the paper . . . to get the news. And it will be full of news. Your copy will be in direct competition for attention with reports of the most dramatic events the world has experienced in the past twenty-four hours. Indeed, the pages of your newspaper are nothing more or less than a succession of stages upon which will be played to-morrow morning a succession of dramatic offerings . . . a great international conference in session, the latest divorce case, a fashionable society wedding, Stock Exchange quotations—a championship being decided in a squared ring. . . . Folks buy papers not to read advertisements, but to read news. Then give them news—in your page as well as in the other pages. Give them the news of your store, your product, your service, your prices, and make it as newsy as news can be made (22).

Again, an advertising director analyses the success of the copy for a car, the Playboy:

> Not the technical facts about the cylinders and wheelbase, the horsepower and gas consumption; but about the thrill of the open road is his story—the power of speed that the Playboy gives to the body of the man or woman at the wheel, the great

outdoors where dull care cannot follow. That is what sells more cars, and makes one yearn for the car that is so written about (22).

And here is a similar prescription applied to a piece of furniture:

'Night Time.' The big ———— before the open fire. Beauty in its flowing graceful lines. Elegance in its rich subdued colourings. Lazy, luxurious comfort in its deep, soft cushioning. Flickering light and dying embers. The closed book and the sleepy yawn. Then sleep, deep, restful slumber, in a wide, soft, luxuriously comfortable bed. Concealed in daytime—ready at a moment's need.

It is in the fields of food, health and medicine that advertising exploits the indirect lie most successfully. In discussing the frequent success of the *suggestio falsi*, Miss Sayers records an experience of her own:

I was once concerned with advertising (among other things) a certain adjunct to diet which we will cautiously designate by the expression ————. A university man of my acquaintance was put on a special regimen by his physician, who gave him a list of edible substances arranged in ascending order of their nutritive content. His wife (also university-educated) remarked to me triumphantly: 'And what do you think stood at the top of the list? Why, ———— marked "No nutritive content whatever!"' 'Well,' said I, 'and whoever said it had?' 'All your advertisements.' I replied, 'Oh, no! Never, not once. It is true that the word "nutrition" occurs from time to time in the advertisements of ————, but we never claimed that ———— contained nourishment. If we did, we might find ourselves in gaol. ———— is everything that we claim for it; it is derived from the source we name; it produces such effects as we assert; it is in fact a stimulant (though it has nothing to do with alcohol) and as such it has its value; but if we have ever said that ———— is nourishing, you may put me in the pillory and pelt me with rotten eggs' (16).

And it is true that not only the poor and ill-educated but also the comparatively well-to-do and apparently enlightened are taken in by the copy written for tonic wines and patent 'foods'. People who are sceptical about propaganda and contemptuous of advertising can be found taking capsules and contents of bottles to remedy a state of 'nerves' or being run down. This is testified by personal observation and by the presence of advertisements for tonics and patent medicines in papers such as the *Observer*, *Daily Telegraph*, and *Spectator*. To some readers the method outlined in the quotation is evident enough; and it is perhaps a little surprising that so distinguished an exponent of the Christian faith as Miss Sayers misses the opportunity of criticising the advertising ethos and the doctrine of *caveat emptor*.

Every age of man is catered for by the vendors of proprietary products, many of which are useful in a strictly limited field, but perhaps worse than useless in the hands of uncritical and uninformed users. For infants, for example, there are proprietary baby foods properly administered only to babies with their digestions weakened by disease or mismanagement. About these some doctors make the following observations:

> The common use of these foods in the nurseries of healthy children has been unfortunate. Many babies carefully fed up to 8 or 9 months, and then in good health, decline from the time these starchy foods are freely allowed. Weight is rapidly accumulated, but it is not a natural or a healthy growth. At a time when bone and muscle development is all important, these patent foods produce fat and bulky children prone to weakness on their limbs and laxity in their joints. Their use should be confined to medical prescription, and once their purpose is achieved they should be discontinued (38).

As the child gets older, its parents are exhorted to dose it with laxatives; some parents administer a weekly dose, and a vicious habit is formed. These medicines often impart information about human physiology and health, sometimes questionable, but when true carefully selected so as to disguise the real causes and cure (appropriate food and exercise in most cases) of constipation. This should be recognised by the Ministries of Food and Health; the former has done useful propaganda over the limited field of diet, and it might continue, under an enlightened government, to impart really valuable health education. But it would of course tread on the sacred toes of the vested interests. Oranges are rightly reserved for children and fruit-juice distributed free, but much of the benefit will be lost if parents say to themselves, as one said to the writer's wife, 'The fruit shortage doesn't worry me, I just give her fruit salts.' The speaker was closely echoing the content of an advertisement for a saline, directed at parents; and whether or not the copywriter intended it, a parent was being rather cruelly misled..

As the adolescent grows up, he meets with the assaults and suggestions of the brewers. They know that the long-term fall in the consumption of beer is due amongst other causes to the fact that the young are kept out of pubs by competing attractions such as bicycling, motor-bicycles, games and clubs. So much of their propaganda associates beer-drinking with outdoor activities and claims health-giving qualities for their product. And it is true that beer is a source of energy; but the advertisements do not mention that to produce energy it requires vitamin B^1, and that much drinking will produce a shortage of B^1. Beer again is a food, of a sort, with 184 calories per pint (39)—compared to 1,857 calories in a pound of white sugar (40). It may be that these claims are not taken very seriously; the Ministry of Labour Report on the cost of living in 9,000 homes of the £250 a year class (published 15 January 1941) shows that the average industrial family only spends $9\frac{1}{4}$d. a week on 'drink (beer, mineral waters, etc.)'. The *Brewers' Almanack* on the other hand shows an expenditure of £4 approx. per head of population per year, or eight times as much as is shown in the family returns. Sir F. Gowland Hopkins declared that in many cases the husband's expenditure on beer reduces the wife's ability to buy adequate food for the family:

> This expenditure is seldom given among the figures of a family budget. It is true that the beer-drinker usually consumes it simply because he likes it. . . . It is nevertheless unfair, and even cruel, that propaganda, subtle, suggestive and intensive, should endeavour to persuade the worker that his beer should make him more robust and increases the power of his muscles; thus tempting him to increase consumption, and helping to salve his conscience when he knows that his expenditure on it is beyond his means (41).

And when we read advertisements about beer being made from hops and barley 'grown in our native earth' we should remember that 'the trade broke up the co-marketing hop board which the struggling British farmer established a few years ago, and the trade imports foreign hops and barley which go to make the good British hogswash that is pumped from the beer engines' (42).

People of all ages are exhorted by advertisements to take this or that proprietary food as a necessary means to good health. Some, though not essential, are valuable—Bemax and Marmite among them—and contain all that is claimed for them. Most are expensive, some are of unknown composition and marketed with unsubstantiated claims. The advertising emphasises the elements which a certain food contains, but fails to mention other foods which contain the same substances in larger quantities at a lower price. Selections of facts and extracts from scientific articles are arranged to suggest that the product is recommended by authorities.

> You who are Underweight, Run-down, Anaemic, Nervy, Suffering from Stomach Trouble, Rheumatism. . . . 20 Million

D

People in Britain are Malnourished! Unbelievable but true: this is the report of a committee of eminent physicians appointed by the League of Nations (Obtainable for 2s.). Even if you eat lots of food, you can still suffer from Malnourishment, which means lack of Vitamins, Minerals and Iodine in the blood and glands. . . . How to replenish the system with all these precious Minerals, Vitamins and Iodine, has been a subject of long investigation. 4 years ago Science solved this problem in a very simple manner. It discovered a Kelp in the Pacific . . .

Even when they have useful properties, proprietary products rarely have any advantage over rightly chosen food. In war time a healthy adult can obtain all the food necessary to maintain excellent health without buying anything in a branded packet. A balanced diet needs no patent foods or vitamin tablets. 'The addition of synthetic vitamins to the diet may be justifiable only as a temporary measure in the case of those who are too poor to buy fresh food, of those who are too ignorant to know fresh food, and of those who are too mean to pay the price of fresh food' (43).

Owing to the habit of eating tinned foods there was a need before the war for many families to supplement their diet by vitamin concentrates. But some of the preparations offered as preventives and remedies for deficiency diseases claimed to have abundant supplies of all known vitamins, a claim made by no reputable firms. The latter too check the stability of the vitamins in their laboratories, but they have to compete with rogue advertisers exploiting public ignorance by pushing products which may be no use at all. It is characteristic of the snatchpenny vitamin pills that they do not state the amount of the vitamins they are said to contain. Even if they do offer statistics, advertisements in this field normally misuse scientific data for their own ends; they give figures, but not in a form allowing the reader to make a comparison with other products. When taken by adults, there may be no worse result from such preparations than a waste of money, 'but there is no guarantee that they will not be used by mis-guided parents to protect children against the danger of rickets, and in this case misplaced confidence may result in irreparable damage.' (A. J. Clark, Professor of Pharmacology and Materia Medica in the University of Edinburgh, in his FACT on *Patent Medicines*. This is one of the best short books on the topics we are discussing. If it is unobtainable, the reader is recommended to get hold of *Parliamentary Debates, Official Report*, House of Commons, for 8 July 1941 (H.M.S.O., 6d.).) In no field is the advertisers' assertion that the dishonest advertisement is always found out so derisory as in the food and medicine market. Here the ignorance of the public, including thousands of *soi-disant* enlightened persons, is enormous, and accordingly most profitable to exploit. Professor Clark's book should be read if possible; and for a simple explanation of the principles of diet, and a list of the vitamins and so on contained in natural and pro-prietary foods, Dr. Bourne's *Nutrition and the War* (C.U.P., 3s. 6d.) is admirable. So powerful has been the propaganda of commercial interests that re-education of the public is going to be long and difficult.

Another example should be given of the misinformation disseminated by advertisements, in this case for meat extracts. They are aimed especially at those who have invalids and convalescents in their care, and their worst result is to persuade a poor person to scrape her savings to buy some stuff in a bottle, which is possibly devoid of nourishment, and rather worse than useless in that it prevents a patient from having the really nourishing food which would cost less. The substances recommended in the advertisements by benevolent doctors to anxious wives and mothers probably 'contain negligible amounts of protein fat and carbohydrates; they provide practically no energy. Most of them, however, are valuable sources of phosphorus. Vitamins are probably negligible' (39). A doctor once told the writer that the valuable part of the meat never went into the bottle but was sold for pig-food; and a nurse said that her great difficulty was to prevent these extracts being fed to convalescents. In Prof. Clark's view the worst harm comes 'from subjecting the public to a steady stream of misinformation regarding the elementary laws of health'.

Under this last heading too should come all the fallacies inculcated by the vendors of tooth-pastes, disinfectants and soap. All that tooth-pastes can do is to keep the teeth clean and the mouth alkaline for a time, and some do not claim anything else. But many imply that they can cure pyorrhœa, improve the gums, check decay and kill germs. (They would do a good deal of damage to the mouth if they could kill germs.) They produce evidence of laboratory tests showing the efficacy of the preparation in doing this or that; but what happens in a laboratory and a test-tube will not necessarily happen also in the very different conditions that obtain in the mouth. Some of them, too, imply that tooth-paste will obviate visits to the dentist, and thus prevent people from getting the correct diagnosis and treatment; but the more honest producers make it clear that regular visits to a dentist are necessary. Soap advertising also offers some interesting information ('The average person gets rid of as much as $1\frac{1}{2}$ pints of perspiration every day. It's one of nature's ways of ridding the system of impurities'), omitting the fact that it is possible to use too much soap and take too many baths. Nor is it true that 'antiseptic' and 'disinfectant' soap destroy more bacteria than other soaps (44). The powers of disinfectants themselves are greatly exaggerated, and much play is made with results gained in a particular laboratory test of disinfectants, known as the Rideal-Walker test, which 'is of little value as an accurate index of the potency of a disinfectant under practical conditions' (44).

Many of the foods and medicines already described come under the heading of patent medicines proper, but before we survey this field mention should be made of the Health Institute type of advertisement, wherein a medicine or course of treatment is given the backing of what appears to be a disinterested body or public institution. Before the present war there were about thirty of these in London, trading on the gullibility of the public and claiming to cure a wide range of diseases by a limited range of treatment. They emphasise their success in hopeless cases, usually with the help of testimonials without addresses. Sometimes they have a 'Principal' with what appear to be scientific and medical qualifications; one such was said to be the author of a number of impressive-sounding books—but neither his name nor his books are listed in the *Reference Catalogue of Current Literature* for 1940. They probably prevent serious cases from having proper attention, and they undoubtedly waste much of the consumer's money on futile treatment. They are quick to seize on anything apparently new, especially if it is a discovery of a foreign doctor—the implication being that British doctors are behind the times and that only from the advertisers can the new treatment be obtained. Some of the health institutes still rely on the 'native drug' on which obscure tribes depend for their health and vitality, brought back for the benefit of civilised peoples by intrepid explorers, etc. Some advertisements appeal at the witch doctor level and even a product of known composition with a certain limited efficacy has found it profitable to carry on an expensive campaign over years, based on the idea that earlier, 'primitive' peoples had a secret of health and beauty which we have lost. Advertisements for institutes of health and stamina, for hair culture societies, for colleges of endocrinology, buy space in papers—such as the *Daily Telegraph*—whose readers would claim to be educated, as well as in the mass-circulation sheets. A high degree of susceptibility to advertising is not confined to any class.

This last point would have to be substantiated with some

evidence of the kind given by Prof. A. V. Hill when the Pharmacy and Medicines Bill was considered in the House of Commons (see Appendix A), if any reader of this book finds that too much space is being given to discussing what are, to him, obvious quacks and frauds. It is clear, too, that to many advertising men they are quacks and frauds, to judge by the uneasy way in which the spokesmen of advertising pass over the subject. Some omit it, others imply that the jungle is being cleared and the rogues will soon be out of business. Sir Charles Higham (17) introduced the charming argument that if there had been no advertised patent medicines there would have been no legislation requiring the publication of formulas, no measures against adulteration. (Thank God for small-pox, it gave us vaccination.) He also claimed a 'simple curative basis' for all proprietary medicines. Dr. Harry Roberts indicts the Press as well:

> Nothing is more characteristic of our national cant than the publication in newspapers, whose editorial pronouncements are unctuous in their moral rectitude, of advertisements the purpose of which is—and is known by the proprietors and editors of these papers to be—the defrauding of the public. And the offence is the more inexcusable in that the victims at whom these poisoned shafts are aimed are, for the most part, the simple, the poor and the suffering. . . . The manufacturers and vendors of these preparations, together with those who advertise their products and the owners of the newspapers which publish the advertisements, so far from being imprisoned or fined, are not infrequently honoured with knighthoods or peerages (45).

The *Daily Express* used to publish a guarantee that 'retail trade advertisements appearing in its columns contain no untrue or misleading statements'. And then the last of several paragraphs of conditions and qualifications provided that 'Advertisements of perishable goods, patent medicines or specifics, housing, buildings, finance, provisions, livestock and personal service of any description are excepted from this guarantee'. The Advertising Association too has an investigation department 'to detect and prevent fraudulent and improper advertising of every kind'. It has effected some improvements. But so far as I know it has not prevented the appearance in million-sale papers represented on the Advertising Association of such claims as: 'Internal and external growths. Wonderful . . . disperses bodily growths without operation.' 'Will quickly end the pain and danger of kidney trouble.' And so on, *ad nauseam*.

It would need very strong concerted action by the Press to refuse patent medicine announcements, because they are the source in peace time of about £3,000,000 a year in advertising revenue (6). This has shown a steady increase; the 1914 Select Committee estimated that secret remedies spent £2,000,000 a year on advertising. I have seen the figure of £5,000,000 given for 1936. The firms concerned can afford a great deal for this purpose as their manufacturing costs are comparatively small; so anything from a quarter to a half of the retail price is accounted for in this way. Their turnover is £30,000,000 a year ('Hansard', 8 July 1941), or £20 to £28 millions a year according to the *Economist* (12 June 1937). A single firm has recorded profits of over £1,000,000 a year on several occasions. The country pays more for its patent medicines than it does for all its hospital services, and spends on them about ten or twelve times the value of drugs prescribed under the National Health Insurance scheme. And as Lord Horder noted in the House of Lords in 1938, 'for every £100 which the Government spent on making the people health-conscious the quack-medicine-mongers paid £1,000 in making them disease-conscious.' Ill-health (according to the PEP *Report on British Health Services*) costs the country about £285,000,000 a year; but only £13,250,000 is spent on preventive measures —health officers, maternity and child welfare centres.

There are six main objections to the traffic in patent medicines: (a) many are useless, (b) they are very expensive, (c) some are habit-forming, (d) they prevent the patient from taking proper advice, (e) some are dangerous or deadly, (f) they spread misinformation. To discuss these briefly in turn:

(a) To prove the futility of patent medicines as cures we have to rely on medical testimony; and Lord Horder and others have condemned them so positively that little need be added here. Either they claim to cure diseases which are incurable—as I am writing I have come across 'cures' for diabetes and fits in a single issue of an annual publication for 1941; or they imply that they can cure diseases which can be remedied by nothing so simple as a dose out of a bottle. In fact the value of drugs is limited: they are sometimes useful in the treatment of certain symptoms. For example, morphia relieves pain; aspirin will ease a headache; scopolamine will induce sleep; phenolphthalein will temporarily overcome constipation; iron is good for anæmia; strychnine is a useful tonic; bromides act as a check on fits, etc. But these drugs do not cure the trouble which caused the symptoms complained of by the patient.

(b) One of the best known of all patent medicines—harmless and unobjectionable, according to Prof. Hill—was recently sold at 1s. 1½d. a box, with the famous slogan about its being worth 21s. a box. Its constituents are worth one half of one farthing—aloes, ginger and soap. A well-known ointment for curing every kind of skin trouble consists of paraffin wax, resin and eucalyptus, and sells at fifty times the cost of its ingredients. These are innocuous enough, but the libel laws make it impossible to mention more startling cases. The objection to all patent medicines is that they remove from the sick and poor money which is badly needed for food and clothing. As the PEP *Health Report* said:

It is questionable whether persons with small incomes wishing to protect or to recover health ought to be exposed to the full battery of a modern publicity machine operating with the utmost skill to produce a maximum profit for the manufacturer. Each shilling spent on a preparation worth 2d., or even minus a shilling, is a drag on the national health effort.

(c) Mild examples of habit-forming by advertisement are supplied by the laxatives ('Twice a day is nature's way') which imply that it is normal and desirable to take laxatives. Or they may create a disease consciousness—for example by capitalising war weariness and insisting 'If you cannot do your job and find it difficult to go to sleep, take two of our tablets . . .'—and turn healthy people into hypochondriacs by suggesting that they have an illness, of which they may have symptoms that fit in with the advertisement. And the advertisements of medicated wines have started the habit of taking alcohol even in teetotalers.

(d) The most serious of all objections to quack medicines, according to Prof. Clark, is that their advertisements encourage self-medication as a substitute for adequate treatment and they probably do more harm in this than in any other manner. The Pharmacy and Medicines Bill should put an end to the worst examples, such as the case of a patient (cited by Sir Ernest Graham Little in the debate on the Bill) suffering from inoperable cancer. He consulted a notorious cancer quack, who pretended that he could cure cancer by drugs. He was given two powders and charged 15 guineas. He died two days later, after taking one of the powders. The coroner ordered an inquest, and the county analyst reported that both powders were cane sugar only. The almost homicidal claim to cure diabetes by drugs will also be ended, but a number of other frauds, such as certain aids to the deaf, will not be checked, though they cause delay in seeking proper diagnosis.

(e) Some of the danger of being poisoned by secret remedies has been removed by Schedule 4 of the Poisons List and by the Pharmacy and Medicines Bill. Now included in the former is dinitrophenol, a drug much used for slimming in America, but now in this country only obtainable on medical prescription. In the U.S.A., however, six cases of blindness due to use of the drug were reported in one issue of an American Medical Journal according to the *British Medical Journal;* the poison also causes pricking, numbness and pain. It used to be said that a cure for smoking caused impotence, but it has not been possible to check this. Prof. Clark in his monograph gives other examples of poisonous drugs, but it seems that the danger in this country is less than it has been.

(*f*) There seems little purpose in the campaigns respectively of the Ministries of Food and of Health to educate the public in right diet and the prevention of colds and 'flu, and in the peace-time drives for national fitness, if a more sustained and powerful pressure is kept up to misinform people about health and the way their bodies work. Isolated facts discovered when advances are made in the science of diet and in the maintenance of health are seized upon, torn from their context and used as pegs on which to hang a fabric of misrepresentation. Phosphorus and proteins are necessary— so an advertisement announces that 'the one basic principle of health is that the blood and nervous systems must be fed regularly with organic phosphorus and proteid'. It continues: 'To the average man and woman————is as necessary as sunshine. You can live without it, but you cannot get the most out of life.' It is true that adults need 1·3 grains of phosphorus a day, but it is not true that the advertised product is the cheapest and best source of the mineral; it is best provided by milk, cheese, egg yolk and almonds. In the same way the facts that iron, certain quantities of vitamins, and calories are necessary in food; that rheumatism and indigestion are associated with an excess of acid; that a gland must secrete hormones if we are to live, are all isolated by advertisers and made reasons for consuming stuffs which may or may not have the necessary qualities. Even cosmetics are sold as vitamin or hormone creams; even a laxative is sold as vitamin chocolate, although chocolate is devoid of vitamins except for Vitamin B. An advertisement in the *Daily Telegraph* claims that a proprietary remedy 'finally and completely ends Chronic Rheumatism, and allied ills'—the latter including gout, lumbago, sciatica, neuritis, synovitis, fibrositis and so on. One might continue listing the fallacies propagated—about nocturnal under-nourishment, acid in the stomach ('enough to burn a hole in the carpet')—but enough has been said to show that an assault upon the public with simplified and distorted and selected 'information' does no good to anyone except the vendor of proprietary products.

As readers who have noticed its passing in July 1941 may consider that the Pharmacy and Medicines Bill makes such criticism out-of-date, its chief provisions should be mentioned. Clauses 3 and 4 prohibit the advertising of remedies for Bright's disease, cataract, diabetes, epilepsy or fits, glaucoma, locomotor ataxy, paralysis and tuberculosis, and of abortifacients. ('Remedies' for cancer and venereal disease were already illegal.) Clause 6 requires on the label or wrapper of every medicine a statement of its composition or active constituents. In introducing the Bill Mr. Ernest Brown described it as 'the first step to reform', and the members who spoke in the valuable debate which followed agreed that it was a good Bill, but did not go far enough. The chairman of one of the largest proprietary medicine firms, at its annual meeting of 1941, when a profit of over £1,000,000 was recorded, expressed the hope 'that the new Act will improve the status of proprietary articles and patent medicines'. So it does not look as if there is any reason for extravagant hope. Indeed, one of the first comments made in the Commons debate was that the Bill was much too tender to the largest vested interests in proprietary medicines and wines. In addition, members of all parties insisted on three other defects.

First, the Bill was criticised because it does nothing to deal with the fraudulent claims made in advertisements, quite apart from the stuff they advertise; by exploiting fear and ignorance they levy a huge blackmail on the public. It was not sufficient, members said, to ensure that the ingredients of patent medicines are harmless; the advertisements themselves should be brought under control, to protect people against their own fears and credulity. This last object was mentioned also in support of the second criticism; that the statement of ingredients on the bottle offers little protection to the ignorant and credulous. It is possible to describe the simplest and cheapest substances in impressive terms which virtually none save doctors and dispensers can understand. Indeed this form of deception was much used before the Bill became law, because proprietary medicines were exempted from payment of stamp duty if the formula was printed on the label. Long formulas with small percentages of unimportant substances were devised, and every element was expressed in the longest possible word. Antipyrin was always called phenyldimethylisopyrazolone. By prohibiting eight particular lies and allowing all the rest, and by giving the public a vague idea that something was being done about patent medicines, the Bill may lull people with an illusory sense of security. A third objection—or an amplification of the criticism that fraudulent advertising would be unaffected—was that the Bill does nothing to check the advertisements of meat extracts and tonic foods, which so cruelly deceive the poor.

REFERENCES

1. *Whitaker's Almanac*, 1940.
2. 20 February 1937.
3. *Introduction* to Exhibition of Posters at Victoria and Albert Museum, 1931.

4. G. S. Royds, *Brass Tacks*.

5. *Advertiser's Weekly*, 19 May 1938.

6. PEP, *Report on the Press*.

7. Advertisement for Cement Makers' Federation, *Daily Telegraph*, 22 March 1941.

8. A. J. Clark, *Patent Medicines*.

9. *New Statesman*, 12 February 1938.

10. *New Statesman*, 6 November 1937.

11. PEP, *Report on the Press*.

12. Advertising Association leaflet, *The Function of Advertising in War-time*.

13. Supplement to the *Daily Mail*, 19 June 1939.

14. Thomas Russell, *Commercial Advertising*.

15. Norman Angell, *The Press and the Organisation of Society*.

16. *Spectator*, 19 November 1937.

17. Sir Charles Higham, *Advertising* (Home Univ. Library).

18. Lord Luke, Chairman of Bovril, Ltd.

19. Quoted from A. S. J. Baster, *Advertising Reconsidered*.

20. Sir William Crawford, in conversation.

21. F. W. Taylor, *The Economics of Advertising*.

22. *Advertising and Selling*, ed. Noble T. Praigg.

23. Robert Sinclair, *Metropolitan Man*.

24. *Labour Research*, July 1939.

25. *Recent Social Trends*.

26. A. S. J. Baster, *Advertising Reconsidered*.

27. S. Rowntree, *Poverty and Progress*.

28. G. D. H. Cole and others, *Is Advertising To-day a Burden or a Boon?*

29. Maurice Dobb, *Political Economy and Capitalism*.

30. *New Statesman and Nation*, 15 July 1933.

31. J. N. Leonard, *Tools of To-morrow*.

32. George Stevens and Stanley Unwin, *Best-sellers: Are they born or made?*

33. Quoted in the *Economist*, 26 April 1941.

34. Stuart Chase, *The Economy of Abundance*.

35. Lewis Mumford, *The Culture of Cities*.

36. E. B. White, in *The New Republic*, 1 April 1931.

37. Consumers' Research, *General Bulletin*, vol. i, No. 1.

38. Harold Waller and others, *Recipes for Food and Conduct*.

39. Geoffrey Bourne, *Nutrition and the War*.

40. It has been pointed out that this is not strictly a fair comparison, in that a pint of beer provides as many calories as the amount of sugar one is likely to consume at a sitting.

41. Quoted in C. C. Weeks, *Alcohol and Human Life*.

42. Robert Sinclair, *Metropolitan Man*.

43. H. A. Harris, Assist. Prof. of Anatomy, University College, London, quoted in 38.

44. John Drew, *Man, Microbe and Malady*.

45. *New Statesman*, 2 April 1932.

46. A patent medicine exposed by the *Daily Mail*.

CHAPTER II

THE METHODS OF ADVERTISING

I. The Past

'Pure as the tears which fall upon a sister's grave.'
(Nineteenth-century advertisement for port wine.)

ADVERTISING in its modern form was produced by conditions which have existed only for a generation or two. The apparatus for reaching millions of people quickly has not long been perfected, nor have there been such possibilities for mass-producing the things which it is profitable to advertise. So that a historian of advertising would rightly devote nine-tenths of his space to the last fifty years. But for contrast and comparison I am going to cite a few of the instances that the historian might use. They show that advertising to-day differs from that of the past in its scale rather than in its methods.

Though we do not meet anything that looks forward to a modern advertisement till the beginnings of capitalism in this country, the historian would have to record, for instance, that books and candidates for elections were advertised by the Romans. He might collect entertaining cases from ancient history, such as Alexander the Paphlagonian. He ran an oracle as a profitable information bureau, and sold the world's first patent medicine—Cytmis, which according to his biographer, Lucian, was mere goat's fat. He is also the only business man to have persuaded his government to allow the coinage to be used for advertising.

There was no advertising in the Middle Ages. In this period production was for use. Only enough goods—and not always enough—were made to meet a fixed demand; profits were limited and the limits were sanctioned by the Church. To risk a contrasting generalisation: things in this century are produced only if a profit can be made on them, the demand for staple products is turned into channels that bring someone profit rather than only a livelihood, and fresh demands are stimulated. We are urged to eat breakfast foods at 1s. a lb. rather than oats at 3½d.; we are pressed to go to the cinema instead of the library. And especially in war time we found that where a small margin of price was fixed, goods in short supply disappeared from the open market to one in which profit could be made. These are the extremes: an economy wherein goods as a whole are scarce, because nature is untamed and dangerous, and produced because society needs them; and on the other hand an economy of abundance, the result of men's command over nature, wherein goods are made because they are vendible at a profit.

About halfway between the Middle Ages and the present lies a period, at the end of the sixteenth and beginning of the seventeenth century, when big cities were arising and capitalist enterprise was taking distinctive shape (1). Many 'projects' of the time, for drainage schemes and for making and selling consumption goods, have a modern ring. Thus in Ben Jonson's *The Devil is an Ass* we find Meercraft, an entrepreneur, proposes to raise capital for various projects; one of these was to provide

> the whole state with tooth-picks;
> Somewhat an intricate business to discourse; but
> I show how much the subject is abused,
> First, in that one commodity; then what diseases
> And putrefactions in the gums are bred,
> By those are made of adulterate and false wood;
> My plot for reformation of these follows:
> To have all tooth-picks brought into an office,
> There seal'd; and such as counterfeit them, mulcted.
> And last, for venting them, to have a book

Printed, to teach their use, which every child
Shall have throughout the Kingdom, that can read,
And learn to pick his teeth by: which beginning
Early to practise, with some other rules,
Of never sleeping with the mouth open, chewing
Some grains of mastic, will preserve the breath
Pure and so free from taint.

Act IV, sc. i (2)

At the close of the Middle Ages, as Lewis Mumford pointed out, the home became separated from the workshop, and the functions of producing, selling, and consuming were split into three buildings—the workroom, the shop and the home. This meant that shops became not merely repositories of goods to which customers came if they wanted something, but show cases setting out to tempt buyers (3).

At the same time the shopkeepers found a new purchasing public in the housewives who no longer had a full routine of domestic work and were thus enabled to indulge in 'the ritual of conspicuous consumption' (4). There were more opportunities for adorning the house and the person—a fact most marked in any history of furniture. Function predominates in medieval furniture: in that of the renaissance and later periods, display—for those who could afford it—counts more than use. In *The Compleat English Tradesman* Defoe notes that tradesmen 'lay out two-thirds of their fortune in fitting up their shops. . . . 'Tis a small matter to lay out two or three, nay five hundred pounds'. Defoe also records a now familiar concomitant of advertising, the style and annual model racket:

Every tailor invents fashions, the mercer studies new patterns, the weavers weave them into beautiful and gay figures, and stores himself with a vast variety to allure the fancy; the coachmaker contrives new machines, chairs, Berlins, flies, etc., all to prompt the whimsies and unaccountable pride of the gentry . . . the upholder does the like in furniture, till he draws

E

the gay ladies to such an excess of Folly that they must have their houses new furnished every year; everything that has been longer than a year must be called old, and to have their fine lodgings seen by a person of any figure above twice over, looks ordinary and mean (3).

By the end of the reign of Charles I nearly every feature of the modern newspaper had appeared in the Press (5); and up to the death of William III more and more space was given to advertisements. Here is an example of 1650:

> Help for the poorr, by medecins easily made for the most usuall diseases and casualties, with a discourse proving it safe to let blood in smal pox. Also a discourse on the internall diseases of the head—by Robert Pemel, physician.

Till the end of Charles II's reign it was rare to find more than four advertisements—of thefts, losses and runaways—in a single issue of a newspaper, but in the 1670's and 80's there were some attempts to start sheets existing mainly to publish advertisements, giving simple information about demand and supply. John Houghton's weekly *A Collection for the Improvement of Industry and Trade* (6) prints advertisements in which the editor speaks:

> I know of several valuable estates to be sold.
> I want a genteel footman that can play on the violin or a flute.

Advertisements offer some of the best evidence that a sociologist could desire about the interests and aspirations of all classes which have any money to spend. The announcement last quoted suggests that English society in the seventeenth century was musically cultivated; and it is not an isolated instance:

> I want a complete young man, that will wear livery, to wait on a very valuable gentleman, but he must know how to play on a violin or a flute.
> If I can meet with a sober man that has a counter tenor voice, I can help him to a place worth £30 the year or more.

The informative purpose is prominent in the many announcements of lost dogs and in such simple statements as this:

> Last week was imported
>
> Bacon by *Mr. Edwards*.
> Cheese by *Mr. Francis*.
> Joynted Babies by *Mr. Harrison*.
> Sturgeon by *Mr. Kett*.

But it was not only about useful goods that information was given. The quacks have always been with us, and a contemporary advertisement for a product which it might be actionable to mention has its prototype in an announcement for 'small baggs to hang about children's necks . . . for the prevention and cure of rickets.' As we have seen, toothpastes were early the subject of extravagant claims, and this seventeenth-century example would only need phrasing a little differently to appear in the advertisement pages of, say, *Punch*:

> Most excellent and approved *Dentifrices* to scour and cleanse the Teeth, making them white as Ivory, preserves from the Toothach; so that, being constantly used, the parties using it are never troubled with the Toothach; it fastens the Teeth, sweetens the Breath, and preserves the mouth and gums from Cankers and Imposthumes. Made by Robert Turner, Gentleman; and the right are onely to be had at Thomas Rookes, Stationer, at the Holy Lamb at the Eastend of St. Pauls Church, near the School, in sealed papers, at 12d. the paper.
>
> *The reader is desired to beware of counterfeits.*

In the eighteenth century there were more positive signs of a now familiar process—the moulding of demand by supply. 'The story of cottons, pottery and iron in the eighteenth century is better understood if we regard these commodities as goods which the consumer scarcely knew he wanted or could afford until cheap production put them before him' (7). The enterprising founder of the pottery firm, Josiah Wedgwood, studied marketing methods, sent out illustrated price lists, and opened a fashionable showroom in London. In 1730 another sheet was started, *The Daily Advertiser*, consisting at first of advertisements only. Later some news was added but it always consisted of at least 75% of advertising. After this success, there was a steady increase in advertising in the Press, and the *Morning Post* was started by a group of business men for their own advertisements. (It was inability to attract advertising revenue, not lack of merit as a newspaper, which killed it.) But to the end of the eighteenth century the main revenue of a newspaper was derived from sales (8). *The Times* of 1 January 1788 consisted of a single folded sheet: Front Page—all advertisements, for the theatre, musical publications, concerts, books, snuff and engravings. Page Two—News. Page Three—half advertising, for lotteries, books and patent medicines. Page Four—half advertising, for furniture, lectures and shipping.

Dr. Johnson's observations on advertising in an issue of his *Idler* (1759) are well known, but as they are usually quoted in an abbreviated form and as the omissions are interesting, they are worth recalling:

> Advertisements are now so numerous that they are very negligently perused, and it is therefore become necessary to gain attention by magnificence of promises, and by eloquence sometimes sublime and sometimes pathetic [here he comments on the reviews and inflated puffs of his time] . . . Promise, large promise is the soul of an advertisement. I remember a washball that had a quality truly wonderful—it gave an exquisite edge to the razor. And there are now to be sold, for ready money only, some duvets for bedcoverings, of down, beyond comparison superior to what is called ottar down, and indeed such, that its many excellencies cannot here be set forth. With one excellence we are made acquainted—it is warmer than four or five blankets, and lighter than one. There are some, however, that know the prejudice of mankind in favour of modest sincerity. The vendor of the beautifying fluid sells a lotion that repels pimples,

washes away freckles, smooths the skin, and plumps the flesh; and yet, with a generous abhorrence of ostentation, confesses that it will not restore the bloom of fifteen to a lady of fifty. The true pathos of advertisement must have sunk deep into the heart of every man that remembers the zeal shown by the seller of the anodyne necklace, for the ease and safety of poor teething infants, and the affection with which he warned every mother, that she would never forgive herself if her infant should perish without a necklace.

This is probably the kind of announcement that Dr. Johnson had in mind, extracted from *The British Chronicle*:

A CARD TO THE LADIES

Mr. Gibson's Innocent Composition, so greatly admired for its wonderful effects, in removing by the Roots in half a minute, the most strong Hair growing in any part of the Head or Face, without the least hurt to the finest Skin, of Ladies or Children; he sells this useful composition at 5s. an ounce, with such full directions, etc., etc.

Also his curious Preparation for coaxing Hair to grow on bald Parts . . .

And a product which claimed to 'corroborate and revive all the noble faculties of the soul such as thought, judgment, apprehension, reason and memory' has a familiar ring to anyone who has read the publicity matter of a contemporary mind-training course; and the slogan of a modern laxative was anticipated by this eighteenth-century advice: 'Take as much as will lie on a Six-pence for two Mornings in Warm Ale.' Publishers, too, were beginning to be large advertisers, though the advertisements themselves were not 'displayed'; small type was used and the announcements were of an informative, not persuasive character. The firm of Cadell and Davies, for instance, took a column and a half in *The Times* three times in September 1798 (9).

Throughout the history of advertising, secret remedies and dental preparations have been prominent. In the eighteenth century sea water was considered an excellent dentifrice, and Brighton brine was bottled and advertised. In a *Spectator* for March 1839 there was an announcement for

> Metcalfe's New and Original Pattern of Tooth-brush made on the most scientific principle, and patronized by the most eminent of the Faculty. This celebrated Brush will search thoroughly into the divisions of the Teeth, and will clean in the most effectual and extraordinary manner. Metcalfe's Tooth Brushes are famous for being made on a plan that the hairs never come loose in the mouth (10).

My quotations suggest that there is nothing new in the current exploitation of credulity and ignorance, and that appeals to fear and vanity have ample precedent. In the nineteenth century 'Science says . . .' was often used as a lever, as may be seen in the example just cited. Here is another of sixty years ago, on lines which are paralleled in many patent medicine adverts to-day. Of 'Hoge's Horehound Honey' the public was assured that it was 'The safest and most efficacious remedy ever discovered for all pulmonary diseases, consumption, colds,' etc. There followed an account of Mr. Hoge's early and lifelong study of bees, references to Xenophon and Keats, and a nature note on bees. Finally Ellen Terry was cited as one of its users (11).

The first case of imposition by uplift I have come across occurred in an illustrated magazine of 1896 containing a full page advert for a saline drink. Headed HUMAN NOBLENESS in letters three-quarters of an inch high, it continued with a quotation from Carlyle—'Every noble Crown is, and on the Earth will for ever be, A CROWN OF THORNS,' an assertion that 'The Victorian Reign is Unparalleled in the History of the World for its National Happiness, Intelligence, Prosperity and Morality', improving quotations from Milton, Moore, Byron and an anti-war passage from Kingsley. In the centre of the page was a female bust exhibiting a streamer bearing the words 'Ever Let Love and Truth Prevail', with 'Do ye to others as ye would that they should do unto you'. Then come several paragraphs of scientific jargon—'How to prevent premature death from disease—use ***** Salts—without such a simple precaution the jeopardy of life is immensely increased.' It was of the *** advertising of his time that R. L. Stevenson observed: 'They are the most indecent advertisements I have ever seen.'

In case by selected examples the impression has been given that all the modern methods were generally used before this century, it should be added that the average Victorian advertisement was a bare statement, often consisting only of the name of the goods, followed by a few words of description—'Ask for Cadbury's Cocoa—Absolutely Pure.' Repetition was much relied on. A glance at the advertising pages of a weekly magazine of the 70's shows that very small space was used by the individual trader, the advertisements all appear to be of equal strength, capital letters were used promiscuously, few illustrations or distinctive name-blocks were used, and the copy generally was merely an announcement. Typical phrases of recommendation were 'World Famed', 'It has No Rival', 'Supersedes all others', 'The Wonder of the Age' and 'Has become a world-wide necessity' (12).

II. The Present

The community that can be trained to desire change, to want new things even before the old have been entirely consumed, yields a market to be measured more by desires than by needs. And man's desires can be developed so that they will greatly overshadow his needs. . . . Human nature very conveniently presented a variety of strings upon which an appreciative sales manager could play fortissimo. . . . Threats, fear, beauty, sparkle, persuasion and careful as well as wild cat exaggeration were thrown at the American buying public as a continuous and terrifying barrage. . . . And so desire was enthroned in the minds of the American consumer, and was served abjectly by the industries that had enthroned it.

Paul Mazur, quoted in *Middletown in Transition*.

It is in the twentieth century, and especially in the interval between the two wars, that advertising reached its apex. The nineteenth century made great numbers of things to sell, and had no difficulty in selling them; the demand for a higher material standard of living did not require to be forced. By the twentieth century the basic needs of a comparatively well-to-do section of the population had been satisfied. In a directed economy efforts would have been made to raise the standard of living for the remainder who were inadequately housed, clothed and fed. This might have meant giving goods away—just as the government in 1943 is giving away milk and subsidising food to keep it within the reach of wage-earners. But it happened that instead of an increase in the purchasing power of the poor and unemployed, those with sufficient resources were impelled to clothe, house and feed themselves more expensively, and to spend money on non-essentials. This could not have happened before the twentieth or late nineteenth century, because before then the masses of sufficiently well-off people had not existed, there was no great surplus of goods, and the means of mass-persuasion through the Press and other agencies had not been developed.

But in the years 1919–1939 these conditions were amply fulfilled. There were plenty of people living close together in huge numbers; this is important for advertising, because people living in masses are more subject to suggestion than those living in small, organic groups. The enormous resources that had been used for destruction were now convertible to other purposes. The wants that needed to be filled and those that could be stimulated seemed innumerable. The means of getting at the people—paper, printing and distributing machinery—were available on a large scale. During the 1914-1918 war, numbers of professional propagandists were employed, and when demobilised they turned their attention to commercial propaganda. The methods employed in the advertising of 1919-1939 were not really new. In the main they were variations on already heard themes, proliferating to an unparalleled extent because the opportunities and resources were unprecedented.

It may be said that the knowledge of psychology made available in this century has given new force and methods to advertising. And it is true that professional advertising may claim a close knowledge of psychology, or, as they sometimes put it, of the human heart. But so far as one can ascertain, those who prepare advertisements have only an empirical knowledge of psychology. Successful advertisers, like best-sellers and dictators, are born, not made. One may analyse the achievement of any of them, but the recipe cannot be mechanically operated. There are, of course, exceptions; the detached and cynical copywriter, putting into practice without believing in it a recipe he has learnt from others, does exist. Though it is true that a theoretical knowledge of psychology is not the secret of writing persuasive propaganda, it is certain that the dissection of advertisements gives one close acquaintance with one or two aspects of human nature. This is clear to an enthusiastic writer on advertising in the *Encyclopædia Britannica* (14th ed.), who after noting that 'The control of human behaviour in the purchase of goods is the ultimate aim of the advertiser' explains how this control is to be secured:

Dynamic psychology has disclosed the driving forces of the human machine to be motives, desires, needs, and wants . . . the advertiser tries not only to engender action . . . but also to show that his own product will satisfy a fundamental need *more effectively* than any other competing product. We find, therefore, that such a commodity as a tooth-paste will be offered as a means of satisfying the desire for cleanliness, for beauty, for protection from disease, for prestige, for success in love, or in business. Other things being equal, that commodity which stimulates into action the most powerful motive will win the market. The use of argument and logic plays a minor rôle in successful present-day advertising in comparison with the direct appeal to desire.

It is time now to see how this theory operates. If we are to judge by a number of the advertisements that appeared in the 1920's and 1930's, a negative emotion, fear, is one of the chief influences on our behaviour. It had been one of the most successful appeals in the recruiting drives conducted in 1915–16 by an advertiser, Sir Hedley le Bas. Here are two examples of the fear of social and domestic disapproval, which the organiser (13) claimed to have the biggest pull:

a.   Five Questions to men who have *not* enlisted.

1. If you are physically fit and between 19 and 38 years of age, are you really satisfied with what you are doing to-day?
2. Do you feel happy as you walk along the streets and see *other* men wearing the King's uniform?
3. What will you say in years to come when people ask you—'Where did *you* serve' in the Great War?
4. What will you answer when your children grow up, and say, 'Father, why weren't you a soldier, too?'
5. What would happen to the Empire if every man stayed at home *like you*?

b.   To the YOUNG WOMEN OF LONDON

Is your 'Best Boy' wearing Khaki? If not, don't *YOU THINK* he should be?

If he does not think that you and your country are worth fighting for—do you think he is *WORTHY* of you? Don't pity the girl who is alone—her young man is probably a soldier—fighting for her and her country—and for *YOU*.

If your young man neglects his duty to his King and Country, the time may come when he will *NEGLECT YOU*.

(A recruiting poster of 1814, designed to raise an army for Gibraltar, is crude, but one does not feel contaminated after reading it: 'Spaniards come into the garrison and returning to their friends, cry, "Who would be a Spanish prince that had the power to be an English soldier?" Here you will be envied by the men. You will be courted and adored by the women. Would you make your Fortune with the Sex. Here are ladies of all countries to choose from—Love speaks for itself; and they know that Britons excel in its attributes.')

These recruiting posters were paralleled in peace time by hundreds of nagging advertisements, insinuating that unless you use a certain soap or wear certain clothes you are an object of contempt to all. Typical is the set of pictures conveying the plight of the girl who couldn't try on a blouse in a shop because 'her undies were a sight', and remedied the defect (crime almost) by using X soap. Fear of not conforming with the mob is a fulcrum much favoured for jacking up the sale of men's wear, but I shall put these under a later heading. No activity, not even the automatic actions, are neglected; you must be careful how you breathe, in case you've got B.O.—'Even your best friends won't tell you'; speaking is risky—'Your mistakes in English stand out ... giving others an unfortunate impression of you ... if you are ever embarrassed ... this new book will prove a revelation to you.' Even if you can talk correspondence course English, you are asked 'Is you mental appearance slow?'—the suggestion being that this can be corrected by buying spectacles. But however immaculate your person, dress and general appearance, there are other pitfalls. 'Neighbours and friends whom you invite are always critical of the china. See that your cups and plates are always irreproachably clean—washed up with Sudsoes.' Everywhere the housewife is beset with dangers—'Do your friends criticise your lavatory?' If the advertising age in this country ever reaches the dizzy heights attained in the States, this is the kind of thing we may expect:

THE BEST SEAT IN THE HOUSE

At the theatre you insist on the Best Seat in the House for your guest. But what about your home? In many homes tastefully furnished in practically every detail, the single inhospitable note is the old, out-moded toilet seat in the bathroom. With a new CHURCH SEAT in white or colour you can bring new life to the whole bathroom (14).

Even if—by taking a thruster's course in business method —you lever yourself into a higher financial class, you do not find security from fear; care is needed in buying a car:

OVERHEARD AT THE TERMINUS

[A bronzed empire builder greets the friend who meets him with:] 'Hello! Sorry the first car I see in the old country is a foreigner.'

In death, too, we may be a nuisance to our relatives. A vendor of tombstones nudges the reader:

Most of us, in our turn, inherit the solemn privilege of contributing to family permanence through the erection of a memorial to some loved one. That the performance of this duty be not too long deferred, and that it be nobly accomplished, is a major concern of a lifetime.

Another well-worked seam is fear of losing one's job, missing promotion or doing badly in business:

HEEL THAT LOST HIM PROMOTION

[Small illustration of a smart sock wearing worn shoe.]
He was next on the list for promotion until the boss walked along behind him and noticed his turned-over heels. . . . Look at *your* heels to-day and get genuine ——— Rubber Heels fitted to-day . . .

Or a tired man, slumped in chair, embraced by permanently waved wife, speaks:

YOUNGER MEN WERE AFTER MY JOB

By the time I was ready to leave the office every evening I felt finished . . . younger men than me were coming on in the firm . . . the directors wanted new blood. If my job went I was finished. . . . On the train going home I often felt completely worn out. I hadn't the courage to tell my wife how 'done' I was . . . next day my wife bought me a bottle of ————'s wine. The very first delicious wineglassfuls seemed to put new life into me. Now I've got back all my grip on things at the office . . .

Similar touching themes run through many such 'real life' stories, cunningly aimed below the belt—'Younger girls earned more than I did', 'My clothes were so shabby and my job depended on them.' Many strip cartoons bully their reader into apprehension: Mr. Garth's boss wanted Mrs. G. to help at a welfare centre, but she is so tired with the additional work that she spends all the housekeeping money on taxis home. However, a friend suggests that the trouble is 'starch-heaviness', eradicable by the use of a certain crisp-bread. Result: thanks from the boss's wife at the opening of the centre, promotion for hubby, and advice too from Mrs. Boss, 'Well, my husband says I'm his best adviser *and I always judge a man by his wife.*' From the States comes a superlative example, noted by R. Waithman in his *Report on America:* Joan Foster's job hung in the balance (Picture One). She was rebuked (Picture Two), 'her department had been slipping lately.' She went to her doctor (Picture Three), who told her that harsh toilet paper was making her 'condition' worse. She bought the right kind of toilet paper (Pictures Four and Five) and three weeks later she was back at her job, thinking to herself, 'The work is going smoothly again—thanks to Soft-weave Waldorf.'

Your job may be safe. If so there is always the fear of

failure in love or marriage. 'Romance might have budded on the 8.40—but she noted he had B.O. and got into another compartment.' The girl who escapes laddered stockings ('Here's Bob's car—that means a drive for you.' 'No, I won't go, Mum, in these laddered stockings.') and cosmetic skin, may—when she gets to the dance—find herself muttering 'My romance has faded' or 'I heard them whisper "Wall-flower" '. Typical, too, is the story of Gwen, depicted with all the perverted ingenuity of the artist and copywriter. Sitting wearily in the garden with her husband she overhears whispers from next door—'Let's ask that nice Mr. Peters to play tennis again. He looks so fed up, poor man . . .' 'Who wouldn't be with that dull-looking wife of his.' Then of course he goes over and Dick's gay laughter from next door was torture to nervy, run-down Gwen—she rushed indoors to escape it. In the hall-mirror she caught sight of herself— 'Gosh, I do look old and drawn these days. Can't blame Dick really . . .' The doctor, through his pince-nez, diag-noses night starvation, and prescribes accordingly. Six weeks later: 'Gwen, you look marvellous these days—such a sparkle in your eyes'—and there are other results which I will pass over. Fear, too, is exploited in every family relationship: 'My own children were afraid of me', says a haggard mother; an 'in-law' whimpers, 'His mother looked down on me'; and another harassed woman exclaims: 'My only boy and I nearly failed him.'

The list of intimidations applies to every age and con-dition of life. 'Don't be afraid to be 40', 'Every picture tells a story' ('Thump, thump, thump—hardened arteries may be the cause'), and countless puffs for patent medicines supply examples. Under the heading 'Widows without means' the married woman is asked: 'If anything happened to your husband would you find yourself without means?' This is a favourite gambit of the less scrupulous insurance com-panies. A certain dentifrice used to specialise in horror—

the frightened figure, magnified by his shadow, poised tense on the edge of his chair in the dentist's waiting-room—'Is it your turn next?'—labelled with an overstatement of Hitlerian magnitude that pyorrhœa—'dread disease of civilisation'—is contracted by four out of every five people over forty.

These alarmist examples have taken up a good deal of space here, because they bulk large in the Press and on posters. The reasons for their success will be discussed later; meanwhile it is worth considering further methods of advertising. Classification can only be approximate, because often several appeals are made at once; some of the 'Fear' examples might well have come in the next section.

Man is a 'herd' animal, sensitive to the behaviour of other members of his group, and to their attitude towards him. Anything different in opinion or conduct will tend to be suppressed, instinctively; 'the conscious individual will feel an unanalysable primary sense of comfort in the actual presence of his fellows, and a . . . desire for identification with the herd in matters of opinion . . . anything which tends to emphasise difference from the herd is unpleasant . . . it will be "wrong", "wicked", "foolish", "undesirable", "bad form"' (15).

First come the appeals directed at us as members of the large human group, exemplified in an advertisement seen in tube trains, depicting a dozen stylised business men, bowler-hatted, paper under arm, inviting us to read the *Daily Mail*, because it is 'Carried Unanimously'. Again, Littlewood's Football Pool used to invite us all to become members of the Happy Circle, and maintained a sense of solidarity amongst its addicts by a weekly Sports Log containing a matey message from The Chief. The same group feeling is utilised in jingles such as 'We are the Ovaltineys' and 'So join the happy members of the Beefex Brigade'. Commoner are the appeals aimed at special groups or separate sexes: 'A man who likes his beer is a likeable man.'

This approach is favoured by the tailoring adverts rubbing in the dangers of standing out from the herd; one of Hector Powe's 'Pow-wows' starts: 'Whenever I notice a man wearing a Sports Jacket and Grey Flannels these days (and there are still some who do) . . .' The motif recurs in these announcements for Harrods, Austin Reed and a provincial tailor respectively:

> There is no merit in careless dress even though genius, wealth or affectation should on occasion appear to think so. Lesser mortals know they cannot risk the handicap, so the wiser among them come to Harrods for their clothes.
> To dress badly when one might dress well may be arrogance —or mere laziness—a laziness by which one is unfavourably judged. Who is so sure of himself that he dare take the risk?
> Men in whose veins the red blood pulses vigorously are now turning their minds to thoughts of sports attire. For every outdoor pursuit there is now a convention to be obeyed. To disregard it is to lay oneself open to being regarded either as ignorant or poverty stricken or—very eccentric. Few of us can afford to be misjudged. It therefore behoves us to be careful in our attire.

Often associated with the injunction that real men wear a certain type of clothing is the suggestion that pipe smoking is another mark of the manly man; the lay figures in the tailors' and outfitters' catalogues are generally depicted as smoking a pipe—or cigarette if the dress demands it. Makers of tobacco, of course, use this lever, but its pull has been recognised by advertisers of many other products which can be sold on the appeal to virility. It was an important plank in the 'build-up' of Lord Baldwin as the plain, honest-to-goodness Englishman; and authors, who may as a class be suspected of being unmanly in the eyes of the public, have often been careful by smoking to make it clear that they share the tastes of the ordinary man. It was interesting a few years ago to note that an advertiser linked up his invitation to buy tobacco with reference to the pipe-smoking habits of a popular novelist and the leading character in one of his books.

Though we most of us appreciate the warmth and comfort that come from a sense of solidarity with our fellows, we like the flattering assurance that in some ways we really are rather 'different', or at least that we belong to a smaller and more exclusive group than most people. So we often find advertisements making the dual appeal of 'A Book for the Few—120th Thousand'. For example:

> We are under no illusions—our Balkan Sobranie Cigarettes and pipe tobaccos are not made for the million. We do not want gigantic sales—they would make the name Balkan Sobranie meaningless. For how can a few handcraftsmen and a small family, blest with a genius in blending, hope to cater for the many? They prefer to keep their standards intact and enjoy the privilege of ministering to the perpetual pleasure of the discriminating few.

(I have been told that Balkan Sobranie used to sell better— as presents—in the East End than in any other part of London.)

Makers of ready-made suits and mass-produced shoes assure us that their materials and fittings are numerous and individual: 'Astonishing how a man's personality expands when he begins to take an interest in being really well-dressed, as distinct from merely buying a few suits.' Such appeals appear to work with consciously enlightened readers; a few years ago there appeared in weekly papers advertisements inviting support for a scheme to sell books on instalments: 'We speak to the aloof: to those readers of *The Week-end Review* who never fill in coupons', etc.

There is no boundary between this class and another which flatters the consumer's taste and discrimination:

> Some men just wear hats to keep off the sun and rain. To them the name Moores means nothing. The man of wisdom

F

and taste, on the other hand, looks for that particular name
and crest as a guarantee . . .

And those who buy cars for their dependability and durability have evidently erred:

> Buying a car is nearly as important as buying a house and
> matters as much to your comfort and social standing. The car a
> man drives is an expression of his personality just as much as
> the clothes he wears or the school he sends his son to.

(Incidentally we can see in this example how advertisements
help each other in building up a picture of the Good Life;
this will be discussed later.) This is a type, exemplified several
times in the following pages, which sells a product on such
apparently irrelevant attributes or prestige value. The
method is much favoured by the experts, and appears in all
the text books. To many of us, smoking is just smoking, a
pleasant drug habit, which is harmless in small quantities.
But to the advertising agent, who spends his life in trying
to impart a bogus thrill, it is almost a mystique; 'There is an
art in smoking a cigarette' we are told, and a tobacco 'has
created for itself by reason of its distinctive character an ever-
widening demand among the *élite* . . . who know how to gain
real pleasure from a pipe'. Cigarettes, too, are sometimes
sold on the recommendation that they are hand-made; a
claim which if true reveals nothing but the manufacturer's
inefficiency.

This brings us near the invocation of Snobbery, but
before I deal with that I would like to instance other products
which can be sold not so much because they fulfil the use
they were designed for, but because they can be associated
with attributes or surroundings which seem desirable to the
consumer. Take car tyres, for example. They have reached a
high standard of efficiency and durability, and there is
probably little to choose between the leading makes at
roughly the same price. So—as usually happens where com-

peting lines are of similar quality—we find an advertising agency urging us to buy a lump of tough rubber and canvas on its prestige value:

The New Dunlop 90 The World's Master Tyre
Ensures **DIGNITY**

The Dunlop 90 is obviously a tyre of pedigree and distinction, and its dignified design brings an added attraction to the lines of the modern car.

Of course what the tyre designer did aim at was a tyre designed to grip the road, but such pedestrian facts don't provide Atmosphere. Nor do the lubricating qualities of an oil; so we must be told that it is 'stored in bottles—like vintage wine'. And when we read of a sauce that is 'Matured like a good wine' we are meant to be impressed, not convinced. An odd 'reason', too, for buying a brand of shoe is given on a price list which bears a coloured picture of Norwich Cathedral and its surroundings: 'In this atmosphere of high tradition, dignity, loveliness, Norvic Shoes are made.'

To come to the Snob Appeal. In simple forms it is invoked for many products:

Ladies, your neighbours will think you have paid a lot more than 16s. 9d. for this shoe.

A Mayfair product—at a price the most hard-up girl can afford.

Flats 'which look out upon the gardens of a lady of title'.

Have your clothes washed with the linen of the classes, not the masses.

More elaborate, more oblique, and probably more successful is the type which shows (for example) a drawing room scene, high lights, piano draped with singer, and distinguished audience drooping around in reverent or critical attitudes, with the legend:

IN MAYFAIR

At the hour of Cocktails and Music; for the Matinée, the Bridge Party, the hundred and one delightful social occasions, when an exotic perfume is out of place, Lavender is just perfect . . .

And a variant:

EGOISTE POUR L'AUTOMNE

Egoiste is the scent of the celebrity and the socially secure. It is the perfume for the woman whose frock sets the vogue, whose *bon mot* is quoted and whose personality endows her with an aura not surrounding the average woman. If you can look in your mirror and say truthfully you belong to this coterie, why not scent your skin with the perfume that is a perfect match for your ego?

A few years ago there was a considerable demand for the services of 'Society Beauties' to recommend not only cosmetics, but also metal polish, baby food, cigarettes and salad dressing, while cheap suits were advocated by titled men and soap by film stars. Agencies exist for the supply of such testimonials.

Last century Matthew Arnold observed that 'Royalty itself we turn into a kind of grand advertising van', and recent excesses have logically developed the trend. When the Duke of Windsor was Prince of Wales the Briar Pipe Trade Association wired their appreciation 'of the fillip given to their industry by your Highness's practice of publicly smoking your briar'. Later *Home Chat* recorded that Princesses Elizabeth and Margaret Rose had been wearing hats more than their wont, though the Queen liked her daughters to run about bare-headed. But this example was followed so widely that

Traders found their sales of children's hats declining very seriously indeed. It was then decided by members of the affected trade to approach Her Majesty upon the subject, and point out to her the loss from which they were suffering. Her Majesty listened with a smile, agreed with the point they made, and promised that in future when she took her daughters anywhere in public she would see to it that they were duly wearing hats.

The *Sunday Referee* has recorded that 'The King is worth £1,000,000 a year to men's wear industries in Britain. That is the estimate of trade experts . . . the King is showing marked signs of "clothes consciousness".' And according to the *Daily Worker* the late Duke of Kent's remark, in March 1939, that he wore neither belt nor braces caused the National Association of Brace, Belt and Suspender Manufacturers to announce that it would shortly make known to the public at large 'the necessity for and the excellence of their productions'.

Another lever which works on prestige is best known by its opening gambit, 'Science Says . . .' The appeal is to the ordinary man's respect for authority (the magic of the witch-doctor?) when he needs it to give him certainty, rather than to logic and facts. Facts there may be in adverts of this type, but they are normally so remote from their context that they are meaningless.

First come those that make play with a vaguely scientific-sounding jargon meant to impress—body-conformity seating and muffled pinking in cars, moisture control in cigarettes, the perfume which is psychologically right for you. Many others make a more elaborate show of scientific terms and argument:

GREAT ENGINEERING PRINCIPLE at back of sensational Razor Blade Development. A secret 'corrugating' process exclusive to . . .

Keep them free from 'CLOTHES REPRESSION'. Clothes have a more serious effect on a child's character and disposition than parents sometimes realise. Clothes that have shrunk (etc., etc.) are all too frequently the unsuspected source of bad moods and bad tempers. According to child specialists and psychologists, if the cause of these 'tantrums' is not removed, the damage done to the child's character may be lasting.

You can now use face cream that puts into your skin *the 'skin-vitamin'—the substance that creates new skin to replace worn-out tissue*—within a few weeks.

MARVELLOUS SUBSTANCE BRINGS BACK AMAZING YOUTH.

Wrinkles are not caused by age but by lack of sufficient biocel in the skin to keep the tissues firm and plump. Prof. Dr. Stejskal of the University of Vienna has discovered a remarkable process by which biocel can be extracted from young animals and applied externally. By the use of this remarkable product wrinkles on women from 55 to 72 years of age disappeared in six weeks' time.

Novel and sometimes entertaining information about human physiology is offered. One advertiser invites men to 'Plant Hair Bulbs in your scalp—Hair does not grow from roots as is commonly stated'. But according to another soapbox scientist it has roots and in addition 'Each hair has a tiny oil-well on its property . . . insist on giving your hair the best treatment modern science knows'. Moreover we are reminded of such 'facts' as these:

All of us belong to one of three sleep groups.
The iodine is drawn from the Locket as a gentle imperceptible vapour by the heat of the body and *is absorbed directly by the pores.*

And the causes and cures of constipation, excess acid, acidity of the stomach and of the system would fill a chapter.

The testimony of anonymous Medical Men is frequently cited; others state the number of professional men by whom the product is said to be recommended: 'Writing in a contemporary journal a qualified physician says . . .' 'All the greatest doctors in history prescribed red wine.' 'The important discovery of an eminent British Nerve Specialist.' 'Eminent bacteriologists have proved . . .' 'A well-known Medical Research Body . . .' 'More than 25,000 doctors recommend S———.'

Common, too, are the summary accounts of experiments said to have been carried out:

> Between January 6th and September 14th of last year an amazing series of experiments was carried out at a great hospital. A group of doctors and scientists were trying to find out why so many people suffer from constant tiredness. . . .

All too simple graphs and diagrams, pictures of the intestines and test tubes full of frightful liquids are regular components.

In less crude forms we still have with us the type which reveals that the health secrets of an Indian are now available, etc. Particularly recondite was a full-page advertisement for colonic lavage. After describing the method of internal hygiene practised by the most primitive peoples, it went on: 'internal bathing by means of enemas is said to have been regularly practised by the physicians of ancient Egypt, 1500 B.C., who learned it by watching the habits of their sacred bird, the Ibis, which, living largely on constipating foods, paid periodical visits to the lower reaches of the Nile, there to carry out a lavage by means of the rough and ready enema provided by Nature in its long bill.' An advertisement for gin: 'Hippocrates, revered Greek physician, sought health from the fragrant herbs of the earth. Some . . . are in use to-day—having been proved by science to be of definite health value. Such herbs are included in "the treasured secret recipe . . ."' And 'Away back in medieval times . . . perfumes were being used in the treatment of nervous diseases.'

Sex is an appeal very widely employed, and a good many

examples have already occurred under other headings. In its commonest use it is an example of the use of association, where the product for sale is connected with enjoyable things or a pleasant atmosphere—social position, wealth, luxury and ease. It is invoked in advertising almost anything from cars to chocolates, especially in fields where a number of competing products (cigarettes, petrol) are of about the same quality and price, or where the consumer is ignorant or uninterested in technicalities. Here the working of the advert may not be immediate, as it is in the case of a patent medicine advert, where the response, if any, follows the stimulus directly. What happens is that when we buy our cigarettes or petrol or beer, we think automatically of the brand associated with the pretty girls or landscape in conjunction with which the product was originally brought to our notice.

Many advertisements again appeal to our desire for ease and comfort—the telephone 'makes life easier', in soap powders clothes wash themselves, and to sink into a certain armchair is to enjoy inexpressible bliss. Many, too, appeal to our acquisitiveness or greed—Football Pools, Bargain Sales, and the exhortation that we will save pounds by purchasing 60s. suits. The most unblushing of all under this last heading was the series run on behalf of Plus Two Cigarettes. Under captions such as:

> Van Boy who saved 2s. 1d. every week now has fleet of limousines   (or)
> Was a Farmer's boy, saved 2s. 1d. a week—now owns baronial halls

we read such illustrated success stories as these: (First Picture) 'Up at dawn, wallowing in the slimy pig-sty—toiling for another man—that wasn't good enough for *me!* If *only* I had some money . . .' (Second Picture) 'I only wanted a few pounds of capital for a start—once you've got going

Money Makes Money. Then the master gave me an idea. . . .
I smoked the 30-a-day cigarettes every working man needs.
He showed me that by changing to full-size *PLUS TWOS*,
I saved up to 2s. 1d. every week (i.e. he spent 8s. 5d. instead
of 10s. 6d.). That tiny saving made me a very rich man.
Soon I had paid the first instalment on a place of my own—
became my own master!' (Last Picture) 'It was tiny but it
was a start. I put all the profits back into the business—
soon bought up neighbouring farms—now I'm immensely
rich, own Rolls-Royces and country estates and have rich
friends.'

From the examples given one might infer that the makers
of advertisements regard man only as a bundle of lusts and
weaknesses. But they also appeal to man's better impulses
and higher intentions. For example, a mother's love for her
child:

> Don't risk your child's health (by allowing her to use an old
> wash basin).
> The trust you will not fail. . . .
> If only for your children's sake. . . .
> You feed him well, mother, but are you giving him the right
> kind of food?

We are still without the U.S. Mothers' Day and Fathers'
Day though we have in the last two or three generations
converted Christmas from a festival of large eating and merri-
ment at home to an occasion for spending on presents,
theatres and hotel week-ends. And there was a report a few
years ago that the Inc. Assocn. of Retail Distributors was
planning to make the public 'Easter Conscious'; an official
circular of the I.A.R.D. said:

> In accordance with the decision of the Council of Manage-
> ment in 1933, arrangements have been made to inaugurate this
> year a campaign for stimulating sales at Easter time. It is hoped
> ultimately to establish an Easter gift habit. . . . The year 1934,

however, holds out a promise of recovery . . . and it was felt
to be wise to tie up the campaign with the idea of recovery (16).

The advertiser enlists if he can the feelings of good will,
sympathy and altruism which exist in most people. To do so
is in fact one of the precepts of the advertising expert. Sir
Enoch Hill, President of the Halifax Building Society says:
'Experience had taught that the advertiser got back from the
public what he put into his advertisements in the way of
unselfishness, friendliness and sincerity. Public confidence
was at the root of all permanent success in advertising . . .
(17). An advertisement for an advertising agency says: 'If an
advertiser looks on the public simply as a market to be
attacked and forced to buy his goods, he mustn't complain
if he gets hurt in the fight. But if he looks on them as his
friends, and sets out to gain their confidence, he'll find their
trust means sales—continued sales.' It was of such attempts
that Graham Wallas wrote:

> Young men of good education, naturally warm feelings, and
> that delicate sense of the emotional effects of words, which
> under different circumstances might have made them poets,
> are now being trained as convincing liars, as makers, that is to
> say, of statements, to whose truth they are indifferent, in such
> a form that readers shall subconsciously assume the personal
> sincerity of the writer (18).

So when unemployment was more serious than it is now,
we were confronted by appeals to our generous feelings in
such forms as:

> Buy a car made in the United Kingdom and reduce unem-
> ployment.

'I dare not write home to Madge and tell her I've lost my
job.' I didn't make that up. It is from a letter one of our
'hands' wrote when he got a week's notice recently. Why was
he discharged? Why? Because you don't want wireless sets in
the Summer.

Many of us feel in a vague sort of way that the countryside ought to be preserved; and the brewers cashed in on this sentiment in a series of pre-1939 advertisements, depicting 'beauty spots', and deploring encroachment on them.

Also to be classified as propaganda to secure public good will and to present the advertiser in a warm and generous light are gifts made to emergency charities and Lord Mayor's Funds, and such items as the presentation of a laboratory by Beecham's Pills, Ltd., to the Royal Northern Hospital. The chairman of the company, at the Ordinary General Meeting of 1937, expressed the purpose of the gift:

> I have always held the view that in a business such as ours the best reserve we can have is in our advertising and business propaganda. In this direction we have this year broken new ground. We are building for the Royal Northern Hospital the Beecham Laboratory—and in addition have agreed to contribute annually to the cost of its upkeep. In consideration of this, their pharmacist . . . a past president of the Pharmaceutical Society, has agreed continuously to review the formulæ of our various proprietary medicines and bring them in line with the latest discoveries of medical research. Apart altogether from assisting a very deserving institution, I think we have taken a very definitive step forward in endeavouring to place proprietary articles and medicines on a higher plane with, I am sure, beneficial results to all concerned.

The appeal to patriotism is not in normal times a very powerful one from a commercial point of view. In the year, for example, in which ran the series of advertisements for British cars that I have already quoted ('I don't think it looks well for one of our representatives to use a foreign car') a record number of German cars were imported. But it has been well used in beer propaganda since 1938:

> To drink beer is for your country's good as well as your own. Every time you raise a glass of beer to your lips—you do double

good. You not only benefit *yourself*—you help to keep the country's flag flying.

This is the drink of a free people—ale or stout, the drink of our Nation. . . .

A large class of advertisements is best characterised by the word 'uplift'. They may flatter their reader that he is a person of generous and noble feelings, of a progressive, self-sacrificing, adventurous—or whatnot—disposition, when perhaps he is not really any of these things and does not seriously want to be. They may enlist a respect for literature, philosophy and the arts, which the reader may actually despise, but thinks he ought to cultivate. Or they may work on the vestiges of religious feeling that survive in most people, by using a pseudo-religious vocabulary. An appeal of this type appears in the literature of a travel agency, professing to report 'the impressions of a cultured and widely travelled woman':

I can only give you my impressions in terms of spiritual values. Just let me explain what I mean by the phrase spiritual value—to me it means an experience which causes me to stop and send out my own particular form of a prayer.

Here is a specimen from the States:

The biggest thing about your telephone is the spirit of thousands and thousands of people who make up the Bell System. . . . The loyalty of these people to the ideals of their work is reflected in every phase of your telephone service.

—paralleled by an English example:

We believe that a great business house of high ideals, high achievement, and magnetic personality can change the tone and trend of the business life and ultimately of the whole life of a nation.

It is tempting to quote in extenso from the source of the last example—Callisthenes' column published in *The Times* and the *Manchester Guardian* on behalf of Selfridge's. A particular favourite is the one which hitches the band-wagon to the stars by a short sermon on cosmic instinct and stellar rhythm—see p. 210.

Religious or near-religious feeling is sometimes employed more directly. When the *Daily Sketch* was running a circulation race against the *Mirror*, it bought whole pages of other papers to publish the congratulations of priests and ministers upon the *Sketch* and *Sunday Graphic* campaign for a 'clean Press'. On the occasion of Armistice Day 1938, Littlewoods Pool devoted the front page of its circular *Sports Log* to a picture of the Cenotaph against a background of Flanders poppies, inscribed with a prose passage in which 'supreme sacrifice', 'pledge', 'honour', etc., occurred.

One of the oldest, and still the most effective, methods— that of repetition—has been left to the end. An advertising expert, Mr. Gilbert Russell, says that to a full-page advertisement 98% of the public make no direct response. But

> This does not mean that only 2% of the public to which it is directed acts upon it. No one can tell what proportion of the public receives an unconscious impression from it. All we know is that such a subconscious impression is made and that in time, if we persist, the subconscious impressions are converted into conscious demand. The man who says he never reads advertisements does not know that he is talking nonsense. But you will always find, upon diligent enquiry, that he has numerous advertised articles among his possessions, and that he bought them because their familiar names give him a sense of satisfaction (19).

We find accordingly that some firms have used the same slogan or device for decades—for thirty years in the case of Camp Coffee. When the Imperial Tobacco Co. held a competition to decide which of their posters was the most popular the easy winner was a very old-fashioned but very familiar design showing little more than Players Trade Mark with a short slogan.

It is true that these methods produce results. It is also true that a number of readers have developed a high degree of resistance, and automatically skip advertisements when reading their paper. This may be caused by a general distrust of advertising, produced by such scandalous methods as those of the proprietary medicine men. But because some of us have developed a habit of neglecting advertisements, we forget that their devices are frequently ingenious, dishonest—and highly successful with many victims. Therefore I have quoted actual advertisements rather fully; when isolated from their context their methods stand out more clearly for what they are. A second reason for these extensive extracts is that advertising as we know it may be dispensed with after the war. We are getting on very well with a greatly diminished volume of commercial advertising in war time, and it is difficult to envisage a return of the 1919-1939 conditions in which publicity proliferated. The drive for wastepaper means that advertisements of this period will be lost unless some are recorded in book form; and recorded they should be, because of their interest to the social historian.

REFERENCES

1. R. H. Tawney, *Religion and the Rise of Capitalism.*
2. Quoted in L. C. Knights, *Drama and Society in the Age of Jonson.*
3. Lewis Mumford, *The Culture of Cities.*
4. T. Veblen, *The Theory of the Leisure Class.*
5. Wickham Steed, *The Press.*
6. Quoted in H. Sampson, *A History of Advertising*, 1875, the source of many advertisements cited here.
7. H. Heaton, 'Industry and Trade', in vol. i of *Johnson's England*, ed. A. S. Turberville.
8. D. Nichol Smith, 'The Newspaper', in vol. ii of *Johnson's England.*

9. *The Publishing Firm of Cadell and Davies* (Oxford Books on Bibliography).
10. *Spectator*, 31 March 1939.
11. Bound up in a book published in 1884.
12. Elwyn O. Hughes, *An Outline of Advertising*.
13. Hedley le Bas, 'Advertising for An Army', in the *Lord Kitchener Memorial Book*.
14. Quoted in *The Townsman*.
15. W. Trotter, *Instincts of the Herd in Peace and War*.
16. *The Week*, No. 46.
17. *Daily Telegraph*, 5 September 1935.
18. *The Great Society*.
19. *Nuntius: Advertising and its Future*.

CHAPTER III

CIVILISATION THROUGH ADVERTISING

I. *A powerful instrument*

Here is a culture suckled on the lion's milk of getting ahead by personal exploitative prowess; a culture which believes that things order themselves best under this scrambling private struggle for pecuniary gain, and that the society as a unit should plan and do as little as possible so as not to interfere with this beneficent private scramble; a culture hypnotised by the gorged stream of new things to buy—automobiles, electrical equipment for the home, radios, automatic refrigeration, and all but automatic ways to live; a culture in which private business tempts the population in its every waking minute with adroitly phrased invitations to apply the solvent remedy of more and new possessions and socially distinguishing goods and comforts to all the ills that flesh is heir to—to loneliness, insecurity, deferred hope, and frustration.

H. M. and R. S. LYND, *Middletown in Transition,* p. 46

THE war of 1914–18 saw a great development in the technique of publicity and mass-persuasion, and the growth in strength and number of advertising agencies quite separate from the organisations which use their services and pay for the advertisements. In other ages trouble has been caused, once the fighting was over, by the dispersal of armies accustomed to bullying and plundering. This century saw the demobilising of whole regiments of propagandists, so that there came into separate existence for the first time on a large scale a mechanism built for persuasion and propaganda, which anyone could hire—if he could pay. This has a sinister significance—a specialised vested interest devoted to improving the methods, extending the use, and making profit out of advertising, employing the talent of men who at another date might have become writers or artists, and working without any responsibility save the increasing of profit for those who purchase its services.

These purchasers in their turn were enabled to transfer the blame and dispel any qualms of conscience they may have had over unfair or deceptive advertising. This dilution of responsibility, or dissociation of ultimate responsibility from executive power, exists on a very wide scale in this century, and it deserves examination. Shareholders of personal integrity may live on the product of sweated labour; the man who does the immediate driving of the labourers is merely the tool of a manager, who is himself helpless in a system where his livelihood depends on keeping up profits. In the case of advertising this divorce of responsible control from specialised executive has led to some deterioration in the ethics of advertising—or if you prefer it—an increase in its cunning. In spite of the removal of some of the worst abuses, partly by legislation, such as the sale of cures for incurable diseases, the general level has descended as technique has grown slicker. Makers of excellent products have found it difficult to advertise honestly; and in the conflict of motives and interests even governments use the methods of patent medicines to transmit their instructions to the public.

An example of deterioration is the descent of the cocoa makers, well known for their social conscience, to the technique of the bedtime-hunger racketeers. An American advertising agent, Mr. Carl Crow, has related how he advertised a British cocoa to the Chinese, many of whom drank too much tea and lost sleep thereby. So Mr. Crow ran his campaign on a health appeal. This aroused the Quakerish anger of the English manufacturer and he took the advertising out of Mr. Crow's hands. Now many manufacturers advise cocoa or night drinks containing cocoa for sleeplessness, and most readers will remember the type: 'He landed the order *the night before he went after it*—it was the "deep sleep secret" that gave him such confidence and vitality— brought out the success-streak in him.' This advertisement for Bourn-vita went on to exhibit a graph explaining how the 'body actually needs more energy during the first hour of sleep than in ordinary waking hours', etc., etc. Another advertisement, this time for cocoa—no brand specified— under the heading 'Rejected Again' shows a boy (registering pathos and dejection) leaving a butcher's shop exhibiting a card 'Strong Boy Wanted' and containing a large butcher with a contemptuous expression on his face. After asking 'How can a lad get on in the world without proper nourish- ment?' the advertisement presented a chart comparing the nourishment value of cocoa with that of two other popular hot drinks. To the use of this advertisement by such reput- able firms there are two main objections: (*a*) working on parental fear and anxiety is callous and mean; (*b*) the information given, while accurate so far as it goes, is vague and selective. It isolates one truth about cocoa, i.e. that it is a cheap and excellent source of calories, and therefore a desirable item in the winter diet of those who cannot spend much on food. But it does not specify what other drinks it is compared with and omits to compare them in respect of their vitamin content. One well-known bed-time drink has a calorie-value not far below that of cocoa, with a number of vitamins in addition; the price, of course, is higher.

There is no suggestion that all firms which use advertising are dishonest or that all agencies are unscrupulous. But I do suggest that where human weakness and credulity can be exploited the attempt will be made; and that in a competitive economy where advertising is a main weapon and results are the only thing that counts there will be a tendency for the agency to get away with as much as it can. A completely honest advertising campaign would not stand a chance in fields where so many competitors are hitting below the belt;

the bad drives out the good. Some readers may reply that advertising has improved and is not so crude: it may be granted that there has been an increase in subtlety (some of advertising's defenders would more rightly be termed victims) but hardly in responsibility. However emphatically the advertising experts may talk about Service in public, in the intimacy of their text books there is a different stress. The choice of metaphor (my italics) reveals the advertiser's attitude:

> Poster advertising impresses the memory through its *powerful sledge-hammer attack* upon the mind (1).
>
> It costs a large amount of money when a community is to be *attacked* (2).
>
> In general, remember that while a shot gun makes a lot more noise than a rifle it just messes things up. Aim the rifle well and you get a nice clean hole that does the trick (3).
>
> Of course, the big secret of writing letters that incite reader interest is to find the right point of contact, and, having found it, play with it as does an expert fly-caster with his *fish* (4).

It seems that with those who handle advertising, a taste of power goes straight to the head; and such intoxication may be perilous when it affects people unused by training or experience to the exercise of power. The irritation of advertising experts when criticism reaches them is an index of the dictator-mind—it is notable that some of them expressed admiration for Mussolini in his early days (5). Like dictators, advertisers want the shortest way to securing the public's submission; and it seems possible that in their years of activity they have shaped the raw material on which politicians work. Advertising, too, seems to have taught something to those politicians, not confined to one party, who regard voters merely as a mob which must be made to submit. These suggestions will be amplified later. Political parties should take into account how far people are already conditioned by advertising, and what in their propaganda they can learn from the uses and shortcomings of commercial publicity. Politicians and educationists claim that they are shaping the future of civilisation; they will not be able to do so at all unless they perceive that advertising has powerfully contributed to moulding civilisation as it is. The next section will examine more closely how this has happened.

Very few of us realise the pervasiveness of advertising. Subtle and imperceptible, it exerts pressure on us in shapes and through channels which the most critical would hardly suspect. Light was shed on one of these in 1939 when G. G. Harrap & Co. Ltd., publishers of the book *The Dog in Sport*, obtained a judgment against the Greyhound Racing Association for £395 15s. with costs. Harrap's claim was for the sale to the Association of 1,000 copies of the book at 8s. 6d. a copy. The defence was that the book did not correspond with the synopsis which the author, Mr. Wentworth Day, had previously supplied. In evidence, Mr. Day said that he had discussed the writing of a book about dogs with Mr. Bartram, publicity manager of the G.R.A., who agreed that the best type of country gentleman tended to despise greyhound racing. He (Mr. Day) had endeavoured to point out in the book, without making it a piece of propaganda, that the G.R.A. had done its best to put greyhound racing on an orderly and dignified basis.

> Mr. Justice Lewis: If you wrote a book which was likely to be· of interest to the country gentleman sportsman the G.R.A would be very much helped?
> Mr. Day: That is precisely the point.

Mr. Bartram said that he understood the book was to start with the origin of the greyhound and to go on to justify greyhound racing as a popular sport in this country. When he saw a proof it bore no resemblance to what he had expected (23).

II. *Moulding habits*

The rise of large-scale advertising . . . and other channels of increased cultural diffusion from without are rapidly changing habits of thought as to what things are essential to living and multiplying options for spending money. . . .

It is perhaps impossible to overestimate the rôle of motion pictures, advertising and other forms of publicity in this rise in subjective standards. . . . The growth of popular magazines and national advertising involves the utilisation through the printed page of the most powerful stimuli to action. In place of the relatively mild, scattered something-for-nothing, sample-free, I-tell-you-this-is-a-good-article copy seen in Middletown a generation ago, advertising is concentrating increasingly on a type of copy aiming to make the reader emotionally uneasy, to bludgeon him with the fact that decent people don't live the way *he* does; *decent* people ride on balloon tires, have a second bathroom and so on. This copy points an accusing finger at the stenographer as she reads her *Motion Picture Magazine* and makes her acutely conscious of her unpolished finger nails, or of the worn place in the living-room rug, and sends the housewife peering anxiously into the mirror to see if *her* wrinkles look like those that Mrs. X——— has in the ad. 'old at thirty-five' because she did not have a Leisure Hour electric washer.

H. M. and R. S. LYND, *Middletown*, pp. 81, 82

It is best to start with one or two of the claims made by he advertising experts. Sir Charles Higham says that advertisement-driven industrialism depends on the urge to simplify and beautify and satisfy life (2). Major Astor, M.P., says that 'advertisements have stimulated home consciousness and pride in the home, increased the appreciation of beauty, colour and music, and contributed to the higher educational standards of the time' (6). In fine, according to the head of Dixons West End Advertising Agency, 'without the advertiser, civilisation as we know it to-day could not exist . . . in the development of almost every side of our modern culture advertising has played the leading part.' What civilisation means to the advertiser is, of course, the ownership or consumption of ever-increasing quantities of possessions, the 'higher standard of living' we used to hear so much about. Even on the material plane it would be difficult to show that advertising has brought about a higher standard. Those who can afford them acquire more goods, consume more stuff; so do those who cannot—at the cost of health and contentment, as I shall suggest. The U.S.A. of 1930 actually used forty times the amount of energy per capita (in coal, oil, natural gas, water-produced electricity) that was consumed in 1840. Yet the average standard of living, despite more commodities and services, was in 1930 below the margin of health and decency; millions were and still are acutely undernourished, badly housed and clothed, worried by economic insecurity. In this country, of the 10,995,000 families in Great Britain, before the war 7,311,675 had an income of less than £3 per week. Without allowing for the fact that families are smaller in the higher income groups, this suggests that 66·5 per cent. of the population has an inadequate standard of living.

It is time to cite some concrete instances of the influence of advertising on buying habits, for they are the most easily documented. Cigarette-smoking in peace time might be considered at worst a minor drug-habit, though the facts that in time of war tobacco takes up vital shipping space, employs labour and machinery, suggest that at other times than an emergency the habit is a diversion of energy to satisfy a want that did not exist before it was created. Created it was; cigarette-smoking was rare in England before 1878 when the 'Richmond Gem' brand was first advertised. Since then it has grown steadily to its present new high level, though very carefully graduated advertising was required, especially in the U.S.A., to break down the prejudice against smoking by women. Now one of the Exchequer's largest single items of revenue (£117,894,000 for 1940) comes under the heading Tobacco and Snuff; of this about 65% is accounted for by cigarettes. In 1938 we imported (omitting re-exports) 294,000,000 pounds of tobacco worth over £20,000,000: £74,000,000 worth of grain and flour was imported in the same year (8). The Imperial Tobacco Company has made net profits as high as £10,636,000 in a single year (1936–7), while for two years running the British-American Tobacco Company has made over five and a half millions net profit. Our consumption of tobacco per head of population, children included, is about 4 lb. a year. And in peace time we pay one and a half million pounds for advertising tobacco in the Press alone (9)—we pay, that is, for competition between components of the same combine, or for being told that smoking slims, helps vicars to compose sermons, induces sleep, and so on.

Beer is another mild narcotic, the increased sale of which in the last ten years is due to advertising. The collective advertising of this fluid started in 1930, and the aim is described in the words of a then director of the Brewers' Society:

> We want to get the beer-drinking habit instilled into thousands, almost millions, of young men who do not at present know the taste of beer. Unless steps are taken to say to him that England's beer is the best and healthiest beverage he can consume, to bring before him all the goodwill and contentment the public-house imparts in England, and to carry on this goodwill, we shall certainly see the Trade on a declining basis (10).

The Trade however did not go into a decline, thanks to the expenditure of possibly £2,000,000 a year on advertising; and the consumption of beer rose from eleven gallons a year per head of population (Great Britain) in 1932 to 13·8 gallons in 1936. In the latter year the beer duty produced £55,000,000; in 1940 it produced £75,000,000. Or in terms of barrels: in 1932-3 consumption was 18,000,000: 24,250,000 was the figure for 1938-9 (8).

In eating habits advertising has been the instrument of a change-over to tinned and branded and processed foods. The advertisers have caused us to adopt a more expensive, more elaborate, less healthy and less tasteful diet, not because they wished to destroy the art of cooking and the health of the nation, but because more money can be made by selling, in branded tins, foods to which no label could be attached without packing. Fresh, simple and healthy foods which go more or less direct from a local producer to the consumer offer no opportunities for mass-production labelling and storing. The war has brought about a compulsory improvement here, and it is to be hoped that the enforced education will check a relapse into stupid and slovenly habits of feeding. In peace time the advertising of proprietary foods had been so potent that even in public assistance institutions children were fed on branded cereals which could have been replaced by better and cheaper staple foods. And in war time people still preferred tinned peas at a time when fresh peas were plentiful and consumed packeted preparations for breakfast in preference to porridge (11). In peace the problem of the food experts concerned for the public health was how to compete with the appeals of advertisements recommending foods known to have little value; the exigencies of war half-solved it at once when the broadcast and advertised advice of the Ministry of Food expounded the theory and practice of a sensible, inexpensive diet.

The sweet-eating habit, accounting for the consumption of half a million tons of refined sugar a year in the form of £50,000,000 worth of confectionery (12) and causing a good deal of digestive and dental trouble, may not be entirely the result of advertising. But excessive eating of sweets and other forms of greed are sanctioned by many advertisements.

There is no need to do more than list a few of the habits

which have been diffused among classes which had managed to live without them. Advertising of the telephone in this country helped to increase the number of private subscribers from 535,838 in 1931 to approximately 1,250,000 in 1939. In America thirty years of forceful advertising brought the number of cars registered from 13,000 up to 13,000,000. Persistent advertising by hotels in the years before 1939 was breaking down the universal custom of spending Christmas at home; in the words of an official of the Hotels and Restaurants Association:

> Hotels at the resorts, both on the coast and inland, have set themselves out in recent years to reap the benefit of Britain's changing Christmas habits. Small modern houses are not convenient for catering on a large scale or for holding a big Christmas party. Consequently the whole family often goes away . . . (13).

In the ten years before the war another upper-income habit was diffused; 'the greatest single advertising achievement of 1932 . . . was the way the steamship companies put over Pleasure Cruises. Or so we lads on the inside, with our eyes on 1933, like to think' (14). 1932 'democratised' cruises, brought them down to the £1 a day level, and incidentally sold a great many accessories such as evening shirts, sports suits, cameras, smart shoes and smart luggage.

A habit of spectacular dimensions—the 'Pools'—could not have been created or maintained without advertising. Before the war competition between the firms engaged was fierce and involved a large outlay on the 'literature' which was every week delivered to millions of actual and potential clients. During the last thirteen weeks of 1937 the postage bill of three Liverpool firms was £220,000, though not all of this could be put down to advertising; and the 'industry' is said to have spent up to £500,000 a year on Press advertising alone (15).

By increasing the occasions for spending money and by multiplying the choices before the consumer, advertising has opened up or rendered accessible fresh possibilities of living, according to the more ambitious theorists. 'Through advertising the masses are able to buy and enjoy luxuries that before the advent of large-scale advertising were completely beyond their reach, and as their standard of living is raised, so the standard of culture is raised also. . . . In America they have tried to raise the cultural level of the people . . . and so far the results have been almost incredible ' (16).

But in actuality, advertising is more likely to leave the consumer distracted by conflicting claims on his time, attention, and earnings, to dissipate his energy on a dozen possibilities rather than to obtain full benefit from a few. To repeat the most evident example, authorities on food have to resort to propaganda to counter the advice given in advertisements, and their advice, given on the advertising level, is liable to meet with the half-attention or suspicion that commercial propaganda meets with. By destroying social custom and traditional ways of using leisure, advertising has acted as a potent instrument of change; the decay of the family and decline of the birthrate have been associated with innovations introduced by advertising. Leisure is made the occasion for consuming vendible goods and for indulging in costly activity, which do not necessarily produce a healthy mind or body. All those, from poets, painters and musicians to educationists and club organisers, who give opportunities for the individual to develop himself, have to face a well-stoked machine for persuading people to indulge their first inclinations and take the easier choice and naturally they have not much of a chance. They are trying to push people up a slope while advertising rolls them pleasantly down. They have little to work on because traditional attitudes and sanctions have been destroyed, leaving a gap in the individual's system of behaviour to be filled by advertising and propaganda.

III. *For forming character*

The human type with the 'hand-cart mind' which we portrayed as a symbol of the disproportion between intellectual and spiritual development, has learned how to use the press, the radio, and all the other techniques for the manipulation of the mass mind. As a result he is able to form human beings according to his own ideas and in this manner multiplies his own human type a million-fold.

MANNHEIM, *Man and Society in an Age of Reconstruction*

It is, of course, impossible to discuss habits apart from the people who adopt them, and that distinction has only been made here to stress, by isolating some examples, the fact that our habits are moulded by advertising. This force helps to determine the possible choices for the average man, and thus influences his attitudes, and, in short, his character. That is almost explicitly the aim of advertising—evident in the experts' advice to appeal to the average man—to create a certain type, an easily standardised mass man to absorb the flow made possible by mass production. The work is half done in the case of megapolitan man; those who live in big cities are already standardised by conditions of work and living. It is this character-type that advertising aims at imposing on dwellers in the country and in the smaller towns. Just as 'progressive' provincial towns come more and more to resemble Oxford Street or the shopping centre of a London suburb, with the flash fronts of chain-stores and the standardised facias of Woolworths, so the provincial person becomes more and more like the metropolitan suburbanite. In *The Culture of Cities* Lewis Mumford points out how advertising, newspapers and periodicals give the stamp of authenticity and value to the style of life that emanates from the metropolis:

They create a picture of a unified homogeneous, completely standardized population that bears, in fact, no relation to actual regional substrata. . . . (They) concentrate on fixing the national appetite upon just those products that the metropolis can sell at a profit . . . create an image of a valuable life that can be satisfied only by a ruthless concentration of human interest upon pecuniary standards and pecuniary results: the clothes of the metropolis, the dull expensive life of Park Avenue and the Kurfürstendamm, Piccadilly and the Champs Elysées, become the goals of vulgar ambition.

Many advertisements work by stimulating emulation or by causing the victim to dramatise himself—to put himself in the place of the successful go-getter or correspondence course thruster. If such advertisements are effective, it is reasonable to suppose that those whose buying habits are affected by them will come to admire and imitate the types portrayed. One can observe it in the mannerisms of those who display their pipes according to the ritual of the tobacco adverts, the way in which people wear their clothes after the manner of the mannequins and 'clothes-horses' depicted in the advertisements, and the poses and gestures of car-owners going through the motions of welcoming and leave-taking as stylised by the artists who do publicity for automobiles. It is not only mannerisms that are formed but the whole pattern of personality. Every society has its ideal characters, to which individual members try to conform. It is at least possible that advertising has helped to shape the ideal characters of our age—the competent business man, the hearty padre, the well-turned-out hostess.

In the way it inculcates images of behaviour and the mental attitudes that go with them, advertising may be replacing literature as a formative influence. Advertising does not say do this or think that in so many words; its influence works more subtly and more potently at an emotional level by presenting people, with whom the advert-reader is meant to identify himself, in situations skilfully projected as desirable or not. It is what D. H. Lawrence described as living 'according to the picture'.

It may be hazarded that people are becoming more and more like the men and women in advertisements, more and more characterless, superficially cheerful, concerned with surfaces, shiny cars, waved or gummed hair, natty suitings, Tudorbethan trimmings on their houses. And as their ideas become fewer and standardised, people perhaps are becoming less interesting to talk to; that is not only the fault of advertising, but is due also to the poverty of their lives. Advertising tries to conceal the emptiness and make life feel good. It is as if the forces of advertising had decreed that the individual man or woman must not be allowed to develop his or her potentialities, but cultivate instead the beery virtues ('Strong limbs and great appetite') and the absorbing interests of the beauty parlour.

The human character as advertising would have it is full of the fear of being thought inferior, of suspicion of anything it does not understand, of dislike for intellectual strength and reasoning power. There is no profit to be made out of people who have confidence in their own powers, intellectual curiosity and a habit of thinking. So with the intention of discrediting disinterested research, copy of this type is often to be found:

> Surely the first prize for Higher Impudence goes to those meddlesome people who work out wretched little sums to prove how magnificently a family of seven can get along on three pounds a week. A fat lot they know about it. . . . Most mothers have to spend carefully, and rely therefore on repeatedly advertised goods.

The kind of character that advertising would like to produce will have a well-developed herd feeling, because a suggestion that can be linked up with the voice of the herd will be far more successful than a simple injunction; 'few of us can afford to be misjudged', 'A man who likes his beer is a likeable man', 'So join the happy members of the Beefex Brigade' carry more force than mere commands to buy clothes, beer or meat extract. Accordingly the pinheaded bluffers of the men's-wear adverts and the hearties who discuss the virtues of pipes and tobacco are epitomes of the qualities characteristic of man as a herd animal—anxiety to be like others in appearance and opinion, sensitiveness to the behaviour of other people, intolerance of originality and fear of being separated from the herd. The direction in which advertising influences the individual and the mechanism of this influence will be considered rather more fully in the section that follows.

IV. For changing language and ideas

As our life is now organised it is extremely difficult for the values of civilisation to find expression or to survive, except as they can be organised, standardised, and sold to the crowd. Hence the predominance everywhere of the salesman type of man. Now I strongly suspect that the mess the world is in at the present time is largely the result of the precedence of sales-manship over thought. A world dominated by sales mentality must necessarily be cheap and tawdry, negligent of finer values and remote ends. It must proceed by pandering to the mob, it must be led by men of second-rate minds. . . .

EVERETT DEAN MARTIN, *The Nation* (U.S.A.)
21 October 1931

Everyone knows that the exaggeration of some advertising has destroyed certain words by over-working them. When one wants to use a superlative, its use in advertising comes to mind; it can only be used ironically, and has to be dismissed. 'Masterpiece', for example; book reviewing might stop to-day, but the word would have to be given a long rest, after its twenty years' hard in the reviews that appear in the Sunday papers, before it could be used again with conviction. 'Epic', 'superb', 'thrilling', 'unique', 'stupendous', 'mightiest spectacle of all time'—when these are used to describe the film of the week, there is nothing left to describe the events, of war for instance, which deserve the epithets. The greatest contest in history cannot be adequately recorded, when incidents such as meetings of advertising agents or the use of half a ton of hair grease for the soldiers in a period film are said to 'mark an epoch' or 'make history'.

Advertising has not only debauched our superlatives. It has invented new words ('mortician') and devised new combinations ('clothes-repression'). Mr. Baster in his *Advertising Reconsidered* notes how the modern copy-writer uses language full of

> simple words beaten into new shapes suggesting friendliness and intimacy. And so we get 'piney' soap, 'crunchy-crisp' biscuits, 'tangy' cheese, 'sudsiest' soap flakes, and 'turny-and-tossy' nights (*without* the So-and-So aperient). The licence is large and constantly invoked, and the general effect is that the living language is fed by a muddy and turbulent stream of new words born of the exigencies of salesmanship.

The vocabulary in which our emotional life used to find expression, words with a rich accretion of associations through their use in religion and literature, has also been bankrupted by advertising, the best seller and million sale journalism. The leader-writer knows that his readers have inherited, even in the twentieth century, some acquaintance with and respect for the language of the Bible, and when he wishes to be especially forceful, he uses this knowledge, and moulds his readers' feelings by overtones from the Authorised Version. The advertiser, too, is aware that by employing this vocabulary he can make his reader emotionally plastic; the writer once heard Sir William Crawford say: 'Copywriters must read the Bible, Kipling, Stevenson, and Burns, because they know how to touch the human heart'—advice echoed by many of the text books. And here are some samples of the fruit it produces:

VISION

As we turn each awkward corner and emerge from the dark undergrowth of uncertainty, there comes nearer a vision, lit by our faith in victory, of the highways of a happier future.

That future is being forged now in the factories of the Nuffield Organisation . . . (omission) . . . It is going to emerge from the war years enriched by a unique technical experience which, translated into motor cars, will result in improved standards of comfort and power. *Such is the responsibility of leadership.* For, just as the Government is formulating now the basis of its plans to ease the passage of the community from a war to a peace economy, so to the Nuffield Organisation falls inevitably the task of shaping the future of British automobilism. *To that task it will bring vigour, integrity and vision— qualities without which régimes rot and nations perish.* (Present writer's italics.)

It is worth examining why these particular words were chosen; one can assume that they account for some of the money we pay the Nuffield Organisation for our cars in peace and our weapons in war. The first paragraph is almost religiose, a potted *Pilgrim's Progress.* Then come some grandiose claims, on which comment had better be left to other makers of cars, since the shape of British automobilism is not for most of us of such world-shaking significance; the copywriter's aim is to impress the stature of his client upon the reader's mind, made pliable by the uplift of paragraph one. There is more uplift in the keywords of the final sentence—'vigour, integrity, and vision', giving an impression of manly sincerity—and the passage concludes with Biblical reference on a near-religious note. As I am writing this, I come across an advertisement for Pear's Soap, in the form of a eulogy of post-war roads, opened by the words 'They shall beat their swords into ploughshares and their spears into pruning hooks'. I quote the examples because they happen to be the most recent of the type I have; Nos. 1 and 2 in Appendix B show even more convincingly how advertising makes use of literary references.

In the examples that follow I have italicised the words the advertisers have appropriated to their special vocabulary for exhibiting warm sincerity and benevolence.

> Our country has got *character* and *faith*, and our objective now is to give our manufacturers *hope*—*hope* through the development of the sales of their goods. And for this development the coming Exhibition should be a wonderful *inspiration*.
>
> SIR WILLIAM CRAWFORD

> From other seemingly impossible dreams was this great Store created, and from this fact we obtain *courage, confidence,* and *hope* for the years that lie ahead.
>
> CALLISTHENES

> In every agreement reached in an atmosphere of *confidence* and *goodwill* there lies *faith* in the future . . .
>
> ADVT. FOR ALLIANCE ASSURANCE CO.

Words are tools which are ruined by misuse, and through damage in advertising contexts many of them will not readily recover. If *virility* is shown by an increase in grocery sales, if *inspiration* is found in Goodyear Tyres, *devotion* shown to Grape-Nuts and *creativeness* exercised on behalf of Feenamint, the normal connotations of these words are displaced, and the writer on literature or religion will have to avoid them. The reader may consider that such borrowing does no harm; but one cannot help thinking that the language and its classics have better uses than those indicated in Mr. Thomas Russell's advice to copy-writers:

> Read the speech of Henry V before Agincourt, in Shakespeare . . . nothing ever written in any language had more

H

'punch' in it. Read 'Paradise Lost'. It is as full of ringing phrases as any that an advertisement writer joyfully underscored for headlines. I never read the essays of Lord Macaulay —and I read them often, with loving admiration—without reflecting what a glorious copy-writer he would have made! ... English is the best language in the world for advertising (1).

It may be that advertising provides the real education of to-day, so far as the cultural side is concerned. The few hours spent on formal education in the study of literature, the exhortations of preachers and teachers, are ineffective against the insistent pressure of other ideas. And advertising, together with fiction and the film, has replaced the old informal education which the Bible and the *Pilgrim's Progress* imparted to the 'lower orders' and the classics to the rest. When the classics and the Authorised Version were staple intellectual foods 'men's philosophy of life tended to crystallise itself in phrases from the Gospels or the Odes of Horace. ... Experience taught them the wisdom that flowed along verbal channels prepared by Aeschylus and Solomon; and the existence of these verbal channels was itself an invitation to learn wisdom from experience' (17). If the reference of much of our vocabulary is fixed by advertising we shall think in the advertiser's way; if we speak the language of advertising we shall adopt the ideas of the minds behind it.

Next we shall suggest how this happens and offer some examples. It is the business of advertising to find fulcrums on which to lever up sales; and for this purpose it exploits not only the instincts connected with nutrition, sex, self-preservation and the herd, but also the superstructure of beliefs and conceptions sanctioned by education, literature and religion. It will borrow the esteem traditionally accorded to certain customs, principles or personal qualities and attach it to buying habits. The teaching of the New Testament for example has given currency to the ideas of unselfishness and service; and we find that advertisers habitually employ the word 'service' to gain approval for their activities. My examples come from the Selfridge advertisements which used to appear under the name Callisthenes, but many others could have been cited:

> Among these is the desire to see the great Store regarded in its true light, as an important centre of social life and public service.
> The spirit of service is not a relic of the past. It is not a survival of tradition but a decision of the present. . . .

If we show the extent of our civilisation by the number of things we possess, the selling of the things—according to the philosophy of advertising—acquires the prestige that belongs to social service, and salesmanship becomes a profession for which no education is too good. Typically, Callisthenes wants 'retail distribution on the large scale to be absolutely recognised as a career worthy of the best brains, the best education, the best birth.'

Now for a few examples of words the content of which has been debased by advertising. 'Culture' becomes a matter of choosing a tobacco:

> Balkan Sobranie is not a name which conveys much to the many. But to the few who smoke for the pleasure of smoking— and not because they have nothing better to do—Balkan Sobranie is more than a name, it is a philosophy of living.
>
> TOBACCOS FOR CULTURED TASTES (an advertisement heading)

THE RHYTHM OF LIVING

> Human happiness revolves round simple themes. . . . and its greatest pleasures are those shared. Thus do Player's fill their appointed place within the scheme of things.

Again, the English traditionally admire a 'character', one who shows eccentricity in appearance or opinion; but now we are asked to believe that character is expressed in dress and personal furniture; clothing 'endows a man with indi- viduality and character' and 'the car a man drives is an expression of his personality'. Of course it is true that clothes have always been worn for other purposes than protection; the Elizabethan expressed his vigour in extravagant and elegant dress as well as in verse, music and sword-play. So perhaps one should not be too critical, except to observe that modern clothing as prescribed by men's outfitters expresses little but an uninteresting uniformity.

Tradition acquires new meaning when it is used to provide an aura of rosy light for the consumption of cigarettes and beer, e.g. 'The tradition we honour to-day' (Marcovitch) and 'The village inn is the traditional centre of our social life'. (Beer advert.) Aristocracy is an affair of using branded cigarettes, gramophones and cosmetics; while democracy —this is a favourite gambit—consists in using the telephone ('the democratic instrument of a democracy') and imbibing beer ('the village inn . . . the very school of democracy, where all men meet as equals, where no foreign beards wag, no dangerous doctrines spread').

Advertising experts explicitly claim that they are concerned with 'culture'. Mr. Edsall, writing on *Getting Culture through Advertisements*, claims that

> The advertising page has a power equal to that of the editorial page. Through advertising we can help the great masses of the people to enjoy and appreciate the finer things of life. . . . We can raise the cultural standard of a whole nation— teach it how to live decently, cleanly and happily (14).

What this particular writer meant by 'culture', apart from bigger and better bathrooms, may be judged by the admiration he expressed for the Elbert Hubbard scrapbooks, as described by one of its advertisements. A typical specimen of these depicts a husband—in evening dress, worried and uneasy—and wife, in a pout, returning home in a taxi. Under the heading 'You Didn't Say a Single Word All Evening' the husband defends himself by confessing his inability to discuss 'literature and art' and goes on to admire his wife's showing at the party. The latter attributes her social success to spare-time reading of the Scrap Book:

> By the time they reached home, she had told him all about the unique Scrap Book. How Elbert Hubbard, many-sided genius, began it in youth and kept it throughout life. How he added only the choicest bits of inspiration and wisdom—the ideas that helped him most—the greatest thoughts of the greatest men of all ages. How the Scrap Book grew and became Hubbard's chief source of ideas—how it became a priceless collection of little masterpieces—how, at the time of his death, it represented a whole lifetime of discriminating reading.
>
> Imagine it! This Scrap Book has now been published and anyone can have a copy. Do you know what that means? You can get in a few minutes' pleasant reading each evening what it took Elbert Hubbard a whole lifetime to collect! You can get at a glance what Hubbard had to read days and days to find. You can have the finest thoughts of the last twenty-five hundred years in one wonderful volume. If you read in the Scrap Book occasionally, you'll never be uncomfortable in company again. You'll be able to talk as intelligently as anyone.

This is an American specimen but it has English counterparts. It may be considered to represent the advertising idea of culture and to encourage a rather pathetic kind of snobbery. It could be said, of course, that the aspirant to 'culture' who thinks it is to be gained by a dollar outfit deserves to be swindled, and that advertising cannot be seriously charged with debasing the idea of 'culture' to any appreciable extent. It can be more confidently asserted that by being applied to the sale of books, advertising has altered the demand for reading matter. Mr. Gollancz's firm was the first to introduce large-scale advertising into the publishing world on this side of the Atlantic; Douglas Jerrold, who worked with him at one time, considers that the new technique revolutionised publishing:

The new idea was a simple one. It was to tell the public what they ought to read instead of merely telling them what you had published. It is the same technique that lies behind the advertising of most proprietary articles. . . . The whole virtue of the new technique, from the selling end, was that it shifted the appeal from the book as food for the mind to the book as an elementary social necessity to people who wished to be considered well informed.

Georgian Adventure

The blame can hardly be laid at Mr. Gollancz's doorstep, but it can be argued that the application of mass-production methods to publishing is bad for the circulation of the best ideas of the age. It means that the original thinker, the significant poet, and the serious critic, who at the best of times do not have a large audience, now run the risk of having none at all. There is less room for the significant variations. The original book has not only a poorer chance of getting published but less likelihood of notice by competent reviewers once it is on the market. For the reviewing columns in the Sunday papers at least tend now to be mere flanking matter for the advertisements, sources of puffs to be quoted and frequently active 'drummers' for the books announced. The law of libel precludes the publication of evidence showing how even well-known reviewers have been asked to tone down their strictures or brass up their praises of books from the big advertisers. But there is no need to cite the more lurid cases; anyone can see that the position is as described here, and that the effect on the intellectual life of the nation is not healthy. Mr. Jerrold, as a publisher, explains how mediocrity is standardised:

Once you set out to sell books by national advertising, the books you sell must be as popular, over the field of the potential demand, as any other goods offered for sale in the advertising columns of the national newspapers. And once you start selling this kind of book you can sell no other kind. In the first place, the economics of your manufacturing and selling organisation; secondly, the quality of the criticism; and thirdly, the public taste, will prevent it.

It may be said that advertising is not so much the means of changing the content of words like 'tradition', 'character', 'culture', as the mirror which reflects changes already in movement. Advertising works most efficiently when it can promote the sale of a product that is fairly simple and easily standardised for mass-production. It is properly applied to mass-produced household goods and clothing, but it is out of place in spiritual and intellectual fields. 'True religion and sound learning' cannot be promoted by advertising and any attempt to use it here will debase the object it is associated with.

If religious bodies, for instance, depend on advertising to maintain their newspapers or parish magazines as many of them do, the result is not likely to be an increased outspokenness in condemning usury and great wealth. More subtly, if they employ advertising methods to gain revenue or support for a church, its spiritual function is likely to be lost sight of. Such attempts have been made in this country, but it is doubtful if there was any gain except to the Press and poster interests. Advertising in such a case is an inherently unsuitable method; it may rouse some momentary public attention and produce some emotionally moved converts, but when the emotion has cooled, so will devotion. The Oxford Group Movement has customarily secured supporters by working on the emotions; among these there are many cases of lapsing. It is significant that the Oxford Group lists advertising agents rather prominently among its members. If these remarks are unfair to the Movement, the reader may consider them withdrawn and replaced by the remark that one would expect a religious movement which used advertising to have certain affinities with the Oxford Group—an emotionalism for instance that rests on no solid intellectual foundation.

But it cannot be said that the English churches are so far gone as some in the U.S.A. where, if the impression given by *Advertising and Selling* is not inaccurate, 'the church is adopting the latest and most approved methods of the business world in securing the interest of the larger public.' This book devotes 52 of its 483 pages to 'Extending Church Influence through Advertising'. Because 'Advertising helps mightily to keep the church modern in spirit and abreast of the spirit of our times' (p. 342), 'we should approach the problem of church advertising just as we should approach any other advertising problem.' An agent (p. 362) says that if a church came to him for advice, he would recommend a market survey and say to the pastor:

> It may be that you have the reputation of having stale goods; maybe you are foolishly stressing side lines. It may be the first assistant sales manager, the pastor, is out of harmony with the Sales Manager, the Holy Spirit, and therefore, all the salesmen, the members, are demoralised. . . .

The same expert concludes:

> Above all, I would make my church advertising prayed-over advertising. I would no more expect to put out an announcement of any kind which had not been individually submitted to the Sales Manager in prayer, than I would expect to preach a sermon or lead a prayer meeting without so doing.

If religious bodies are not circumspect in the use of advertising, they may find that advertising is not slow to use them and their faiths. The *Universe* (18) claims in its advertisements to have 'an unmistakable hold upon the Catholic community. . . . Readers trust the *Universe* and the prestige of their trust is enjoyed by advertisers'—an admission on which St. Thomas Aquinas could have commented better than I can. Advertising may not often employ religion as directly as the American (3) who made a lever of it to support the power companies: 'Next to God and religion, the utilities are the most important things that enter our lives', or so candidly as the maker of lifts who practised his belief that advertising should appeal to a man's religion, by asserting in his publicity that 'Successful business is in the hands of Religious Men' and following it up with a list of heads of companies who were both 'Religious Men and Good Steam Hydraulickers'.

Advertising, however, does not often exploit religion so directly. Commoner is the use as levers of religious and near-religious feelings, whether Christian or pagan, and the practice in 'uplift' adverts of borrowing the language of the Old Testament and the ideas of the New; see Nos. 1 and 3 in Appendix B.

Sir William Crawford (3) once observed that 'it is not merely phrases, slogans and speeches that are demanded of advertising men; rather is it truth, philosophy, and vision'; and the claim to supply a philosophy of life has been made on behalf of advertising by many of its practitioners. In brief, the philosophy for society is one of progress in the invention and multiplication of material adjuncts to living; and for the individual the acquisition of as many as possible of these goods. The aim for society is summarised in an advertisement written by Mr. Marchant Smith:

> Almost in a night we pass from stone to concrete, from hickory to steel—from movies to talkies, from coddling to sun baths, from six cylinders to eight! With this world that moves at prodigious speed Crawford advertising is in touch and in tune. Unfrightened by tradition—modern as the moment of its making—it has proved that reward is for those who will dare what has never been done before (19).

And even in the winter of 1941–2 when paper was urgently needed for national purposes, a motor company issued many advertisements, including whole pages in motoring papers, which declared that

The New World is being planned *now*. New architecture will arise, another Christopher Wren. Science will leap ahead, revitalised by the lessons of the war. The conquest of the air will be complete. And on the streets of the new world will appear faster, better, safer forms of transport.

It is natural that advertising should proclaim acquisition as a philosophy for the individual, because it thrives on a steady stream of things made to be acquired. This forced acquisitiveness is not quite the same thing as delight in spending and possessing. In a feudal or semi-feudal society, with its conservation, exploitation, narrowness, lack of opportunity for talent, the social scale had fixed divisions, and there was little or no opportunity for ascending. The different orders knew their status, there was no rising on the shoulders of others. But on the social slope of to-day, the display of wealth in the ownership of things is the criterion of excellence, the chief means of distinction. Thus advertising has helped to promote acquisition to the status of religion; hence the common claim of exclusiveness for mass-produced goods, the illusion of aristocratic distinction to be obtained by smoking the cigarettes which are depicted as being used by a dress suit wearing the order of the Golden Fleece, by purchasing the same face cream or metal polish that give beauty to Lady X's face or Lady Y's silver. As a writer in *Willing's Press Guide* for 1939 observed:

> One of the world's greatest advertising agencies believes in selling the 'other people' copy. In short it endorses—and continually proves—the sales power of emulation. On a percentage basis, the 'people at the top' may seem small, but in buying capacity and emulation influence they merit an entirely effective average. They shun forceful sales methods, but can be impregnably 'sold' by the use of Illustrated Newspapers.

And as the Lynds noted of America:

> It is characteristic of urban life, with its large jumbled populations that include many strangers, to bridge the gap

between anonymity and belonging by the device of overt material possessions that 'place' one. As a Middletown citizen remarked in 1925: 'People know money, and they don't know you' (20).

As early as 1899 Thorstein Veblen had made a similar note in his *Theory of the Leisure Class*, a theory developed with fantastic irony. As he asserts, the basis of good repute in an industrial community is pecuniary strength, displayed in leisure and the consumption of goods; and he argues that both these methods of showing strength will be found as far down the social scale as possible. Where the husband has to work most of his time, the function of leisure is delegated to his wife, and still lower, where no leisure is possible to the wife, the conspicuous consumption of goods remains. 'The only practicable means of impressing one's pecuniary ability on . . . unsympathetic observers of one's everyday life is an unremitting demonstration of the ability to pay.'

There is no intention to attribute to advertising the fact that acquisition is so common an aim; it is significant that Veblen published his *Theory of the Leisure Class* in 1899, before the rise of high-pressure publicity. Advertising found acquisitiveness well established, made good use of it as a sales drive and thereby inculcated it more forcibly and pervasively. To examine the results of this acquisitiveness would carry us too far from the subject, but a few may be mentioned. Civilisation as at present managed leads not to more leisure and greater contentment, but to more work by more people. The Lynds cite 'the pressure of the commercially encouraged psychological standard of living . . . as a strong contributing cause to the increase of Middletown's married workers in a decade of prosperity like the 1930's . . . as each family scrambles for more security and more things in a culture in which one is largely judged by the things one has' (20). Again, social competition, in which the marks of attainment are luxury goods, is a contributing cause to the decline of the birth-rate. Those who have children may not give their children so good an upbringing as they might have but for the expense of a car or second car. Another question is: has the limited improvement in material conditions been used as a basis for fuller living or pursued as a self-sufficient end? Mr. Rowntree's *Poverty and Progress* suggests to some readers that advertising pressure has not worked to desirable effect here. Spending habits controlled by advertising may lead not only to neglect of educational and cultural pursuits and of the more active uses of leisure but also to under-spending on basic needs; in the words of Veblen:

> The conspicuously wasteful honorific expenditure that confers spiritual well-being may become more indispensable than much of that expenditure which ministers to the 'lower' wants of physical well-being or sustenance only.

This lack of balance in the activity of our society leads Mr. Baster to conclude that the uneven effect of advertising in different departments of consumption 'tends to distort the productive process in the direction of employing an excessive proportion of the community's resources in producing things which people can be easily persuaded to want, with the necessary consequence of an insufficient output of the other things'. The misdirection continues even in war time; as late as March 1942 the Select Committee on National Expenditure reported that manpower was still being absorbed in pushing sales of non-essential products. From the beginning of the war advertising was used to encourage spending in a way calculated to defeat the National Savings Campaign. 'Cigarette smokers', we were told, 'are helping to win the economic war by smoking Turkish'; 'Buy a 5 guinea suit for £4 and put the money saved to Defence Bonds'; 'As a help to the nation's purse you should stick to Beer.' These appeals, and hundreds of others for proprietary goods and for big stores, must have helped to lengthen the war by diverting labour and material from the national purpose. One might have hoped that a Government which has been ruthless in breaking up families, requisitioning small properties and disposing of lives might have shown a little understanding of and perhaps a little toughness towards the interests which can afford to advertise in so patently anti-social a manner. But the Government could hardly be expected to take up a firm line when its mind was not quite satisfied about the significance of advertising, at least when Mr. Lyttelton was president of the Board of Trade:

> I must say one word about brands and trade-marks. Most people desire to keep their brands and trade-marks in front of the public, and I think it is interesting to see that in many instances where manufacturers are engaged in Government work they are keeping their brands in front of the public by means of advertisement. We shall give all the help we can to keeping alive these trade-marks.

It is difficult to measure the extent to which the ideal of acquisition has moulded the thoughts of our society; it must by very considerable. Mannheim suggests that even in our personal relations we tend to regard each other as commodities, and Dr. Ruth Benedict goes further:

> Without the clue that in our civilisation at large man's paramount aim is to amass private possessions and multiply occasions of display, the modern position of the wife and the modern emotions of jealousy are alike unintelligible. Our attitudes toward our children are equally evidences of this same cultural goal. Our children are not individuals whose rights and tastes are casually respected from infancy, as they are in some primitive societies, but special responsibilities, like our possessions, to which we succumb, or in which we glory, as the case may be (21).

It seems, too, that churches and universities are thinking in the same mould, to judge by the way in which they erect buildings as an outward sign of their importance. Any really revolutionary political party should be aware that an effective revolution will not be merely political or economic, not only a question of dividends for all, but will entail a re-education to put the acquisitive instincts in their right place. Acquisitiveness is one of the major drives of our civilisation, but it is one that may become dangerously anti-social. Therefore an attempt to maintain it as a goal of living, as advertising does, is unhelpful and unrealistic; to reinforce an idea, which as a motive for the development of society is out of date and won't work, is to set up a barrier against change at a point where revision of our concepts is badly needed. It may cause the change to be sudden and violent when it does come.

Politicians at any rate when they consider the normal apathy of the electorate may agree with Mumford's suggestion that the growth of domesticity tends to substitute private life for an interest in public affairs. It does seem possible that advertising by offering distractions tends to turn public attention from economic and social questions; and that by insistently stressing the importance of self it crowds out the civic feelings, a sense of responsibility. By setting the possession of goods as the scale up which we must ascend to gain the recognition of others, it diminishes the energy we have left for gaining respect in other ways. It is interesting to find an editor of *The New Republic* (1 September 1941), in the course of an analysis of American morale, attributing its weakness as compared with Russia's to worship of the competitive system, amongst other causes. Millions of Americans, he says, have got the idea that the aim of civilisation is the comfort of the individual, with the result that they are callous to suffering outside the States:

> We have managed to turn out many people so insensitive that suffering means nothing unless it occurs actually under their eyes; so shortsighted that they cannot recognise a coming catastrophe until it is upon them, but continue to prattle in the

sunshine like children playing in an open field while a hurricane approaches; so wholly intent on personal satisfactions that they are prepared if necessary to sacrifice a great part of their freedom, their dignity, the ultimate human values of their life, if only they can be permitted to retain for the time being their pretty toys, their automobiles, bridge games, movies, their air-conditioned restaurants and stream-lined trains.

It can best be left to the reader to decide how far Mr. Bliven's notes on the U.S.A. apply to this country; whether, that is, there is any connection between a commercially stimulated interest in tangible goods and the lack of intelligent interest in public affairs which marked the twenty years' armistice of 1919-39.

Writers on advertising frequently claim credit for the raising of the standard of living, and if any rise in the standard where it was needed can so be attributed, one would not grudge the claim. Even when the basic needs have been filled, there is undeniably a real satisfaction to be had from the mere possession—according to one's tastes—of good furniture, radio-sets, bicycles, cars, and so on. But it is time to set a limit to acquisition if it leads to the negation of qualities, interests and activities which cannot be expressed in ownership—values which are the most important part of man, according to ideas to which we still pay lip-service. In this connection the view of psychologists is interesting:

It seems, however, that we may now be nearing the point at which external goodness—prosperity and material gains—will have taken the place of internal goodness as an ideal. Prosperity, as we all know, is a great aid, though not actually a means, towards inner goodness; it is, however, not a substitute for it. And if material gain becomes the ideal, the inner life of man is by so much denied and may itself come into contempt. The effect of this reaction is that there is now a considerable *dissociation and denial* of the part played in life by our *inner emotional needs*. Our need to love, as our strongest security against the anxiety of hate and destructiveness within, together with the problems of guilt which are inseparable from love, and the standards of conscience and morality that spring from our guilt, all suffer from neglect, are denied, and may starve in their turn though material prosperity increases (22).

The last few pages have tried to show how advertising modifies one's ideas. A further point remains. All the conceptions which advertising adds to the existing furniture of our minds, mass-produced by film, press, and novel, are stereos—conventional images of the successful business man, the happy lover, the perfect wife, the aristocrat, the democrat. It is inevitable that we should use stereos as labour-saving devices, but there is much to be said against their forming the staple of our intellectual stock. Many of them touch reality at so few points that they won't work in practice. The man or woman who derives from advertisements and films his or her idea of how a husband and wife should behave is not likely thereby to manage the complexities of living more satisfactorily. Nor is specially good citizenship likely to be found in the voter who forms his idea of democracy on the beer adverts which tell him that the pub 'where all men meet as equals' is 'the very school of democracy', etc. Again, if people accept the stereo of the good life that advertising offers they will find it so inapplicable, unattainable or inadequate, that there is bound to be some maladjustment in their lives. Here is an example; an advertising manager is explaining how her column works:

> The column sells hope, luxury, and the whirl of parties, dreams of country clubs and proms, visions of what might happen if only. . . . If only you fill in the missing link and buy a new dinner jacket, or plates like Mrs. Harding's, a splashing motor car, a glass bracelet, or an ermine wrap. And once you get that vision you don't have to be sold anything—you buy. The column sells wedding dresses by weaving romance instead of shouting prices . . . (3).

The insemination of an ideal of life which is likely to be both insufficient in itself and unattainable anyhow will not lead to contentment. Perhaps it is too readily assumed here that advertising has a direct influence of the kind I am describing, and if it does exist it may not be easy to measure. But I have heard quoted with approval in a sermon the anecdote about the man who kept up his morale in the desert by dressing for dinner every night; and if the implied belief that such superficialities matter does not come from advertising, it is at least confirmed and disseminated by such advertisements as that for Shavex, depicting handsome man at party admired by pretty girl because when out East 'He put on a dinner jacket every night . . . he let the Arabs know he was civilised'.

V. Regression

When the instruments of propaganda are concentrated in a few hands, they may be monopolised by the more primitive type, and then the spiritual regression which has already appeared, becomes permanent.

Man and Society in an Age of Reconstruction, p. 74

It would be easy to suggest that advertising is responsible for a return to the primitive, but it would not be very exact. Advertising may have contributed to the process whereby many acquired characteristics have been shed, and the word for this is 'dehumanising'. It may, of course, be an exaggeration to attribute to advertising even a small part of the dehumanising that has taken place—an exaggeration possibly produced by a closeness to the subject and a resulting lack of proportion. So what follows is offered tentatively.

Advertising and propaganda generally appeal to the three or four universal instincts which civilised man has in common with the savage. In so far as man has made any progress

I

from the merely animal stage, it is by acquiring fresh characteristics. Oral tradition, books and religion transmitted the lessons of experience, until about a century ago when —in England at least—large sections of the population started to lose their collective memory and to jettison the wisdom of experience. Now the mass-populations of the civilised world seem to be going through a stage of de-differentiation.

The users of certain types of advertising contribute to the change, by reminding us incessantly of our animal needs. To eat and be clothed, to evacuate, to take paid-for exercises and have diseases are the functions of the mindless body which represents a human being in the more irrational advertisements. If it occurs to the consumer that a round of self-gratification at this level is not entirely commendable, advertising steps in to provide justifications. This providing of justifications for men to do as they like is exemplified in the advertising of lime drinks (to correct hang-overs) and indigestion remedies; here is an example:

OVER-INDULGENCE

is no crime, and it is folly to suffer for every little indiscretion. Every man, woman and child must occasionally over-indulge. Who can live without so doing? Who would want to?

Hearty eaters can rectify a sour stomach with one spoonful of ———. Smokers have long since learned that the same perfect antacid neutralises nicotine; brings back a sweet taste; guards the breath. Etc., etc.

The suggestion that gluttonous eating and drinking are venial and easily corrected by something out of a bottle amounts nearly to an invitation. We are most of us ready to accept excuses for self-indulgence and self-pity, for laziness instead of activity, especially mental, and advertising fits us out with rationalisations on a grand scale. For instance, under the heading 'Virtue is its own Reward', we read:

A far from satisfying precept in a world filled with so many pleasant things. After a day of virtuous labour a man has reason to expect a more material solace such as exists in the amber depths, the mellow luxury, the comforting full flavour of——.

Of course it is not implied here that the pleasures of eating and drinking have no place in a reasonable scheme of life. But the force of such advertisements is to mobilise and provide mere impulses and gross appetites with status. The minor forms of original sin have a high cash value to-day.

Advertising does more than exploit the primary impulses of men. The consumer must never be allowed to manage his own life; so a pipe-line is laid on to every part of his make-up. No part of his person, his thoughts or his feelings, is too intimate for the manipulation of the 'adman'. In search of the soft spot advertising tries first to cater for us as individuals, flattering us as members of a particular economic stratum, as character-types ('Chypre—Definitely the perfume of the brunette—dark hair, dark eyes, and a lissom figure. Chypre is for the passionate, emotional woman—earnest, and usually of an artistic temperament') and even as owners of a particular make of car ('When I saw your Studebaker parked down the road the other day'— from an American sales letter). Growing more intimate, they send circulars to those who announce marriages or births in the Press; or they touch on subjects, such as the physical changes in adolescent girls, which are not usually discussed so publicly. And it is possible that in getting hold of them young, advertising helps the film to stimulate a self-consciousness about sex in minds which have not been mentally prepared for growing up. This self-consciousness once developed is not allowed to die. Women, for instance, find themselves standardised as man-hunters, though perhaps not often as directly as in this announcement of a perfume:

Woman's deep-seated instinct urging her to the use of perfumes is a manifestation of a fundamental law of biology. *The
first duty of woman is to attract.* ... It does not matter how
clever or independent you may be, if you fail to influence the
men you meet, consciously or unconsciously, you are not
fulfilling your fundamental duty as a woman. ... You must
experiment ceaselessly until your intuition and the reaction of
your *male* friends tell you you have found your perfect perfume.
(Italics in the original, which is abbreviated here.)

We have at various times heard warnings against the
dangers of a mechanical civilisation; and it seems that
advertising is one of the moulding forces and the mouthpiece
through which the ideas behind the impersonal, inhuman
machine become vocal. Regression sets in because platitu-
dinous ideas about people and a stereotyped pattern of
living are disseminated; feeling becomes conventional and
loses individual quality. If progress in advertising continues,
emotional life will become more and more a matter of stock
responses to commercialised appeals, such as those of
Mothers' Day or Fathers' Day in the U.S.A. It may be said
that the life of many people has always been a matter of
almost automatic response to situations that arose, and that
individual feeling has rarely existed; and it is true that, for
many, emotion has run in the channels formed by the
Scriptures, by poets and allegorists, by traditional attitudes,
by pagan and Christian religions. Still the word regression is
applicable, if the reader will agree that as formative influences
priests and poets at their best have been preferable to the
profit motive.

This is the driving force of civilisation to-day, and by
itself it does not bring satisfaction. We still keep up a façade
of beliefs, which come in useful for politicians and advertisers
when they wish to impose some action upon us by appealing
to our better natures, but the less confidently formulated
convictions determine many of our actions. Religion and

'the finer things of life' are our ultimate values—in public: in private, we make as much money as we can. Honesty is the best policy—in print: but in practice business is business. (cf. R. S. Lynd, *Knowledge for What?* p. 60.)

I am not accusing advertisers of being a set of Machiavellian villains plotting to instil into millions of innocents a faith in getting and spending. That is far from the truth. On the other hand it is true that a large number of channels of information are controlled by people not qualified to feed ideas to the public. They are not numerous, but they are like-minded. If their prime mover is profit, everything they hand out to readers will be coloured by the doctrine that profit is what matters. By way of analogy: a given mechanical problem has often only one solution, which will be reached independently by one engineer in Detroit and another in Coventry. In the same way, given profit as the main drive of civilisation, everything else being subordinated to it, the tendency will be for only those concepts, beliefs and motives that are accessory to profit-making to reach the public. Thus it happens that American and English advertising are very alike; similar ideas and plans occur simultaneously and spontaneously to the advertising engineers of public opinion in London and New York.

Perhaps it should be said once more that we cannot regard advertising as an isolated phenomenon. It is a weakness of civilisation and at the same time a means of insight into its failings.

The advertisers of advertising have often told us that we owe to it many of the blessings of civilisation. It might be replied that it has prevented us from enjoying them in peace; a London evening newspaper, putting forward its claims to pulling power, reveals an aim of advertising—to allow the victim no rest:

> Londoners . . . whose leisure is generally restricted, are at the peak of receptivity when they read their evening newspapers.

Many readers of advertisements would be indignant if they knew how advertising tries to get at them in all their waking moments. But it is not enough merely to blame the advertisers. We must secure a state of affairs where such prying does not pay, where the consumer has more conscious power of resistance. However, at present, there is little doubt that advertising, as well as being a mirror of the restlessness of our civilisation, actually increases that restlessness by the methods it uses. Much advertising thrives on discontent—with one's pay, physique or environment—or may create discontent where there was none before. It then offers an escape. But however perfect the advertised life may be in the posters, it is a way of life which could satisfy no-one even if it were attainable. There cannot be contentment in a constant struggle for money to meet the demands of the advertisements, or in the suburban boredom which may be achieved when the gap between the ideal and the actual contracts. High-pressure advertising could only exist in a society which had created insecurity, anxiety, and neuroses on a large scale.

REFERENCES TO CHAPTER III

1. Thomas Russell, *Commercial Advertising*.
2. Sir Charles Higham, *Advertising*.
3. *Advertising and Selling*, ed. N. T. Praig, p. 150
4. *Ibid.*, p. 144.
5. *Ibid.*, p. 5.
6. Quoted in *The Times*, 28 September 1933.
7. Stuart Chase, *The Economy of Abundance*.
8. *Whitaker's Almanac*, 1940.
9. Figure for 1935, *The Economist*, 27 February 1937.
10. Quoted in Robert Sinclair, *Metropolitan Man*.
11. Ministry of Food statement, *Daily Telegraph*, 16 January 1941.
12. *Daily Telegraph*, 29 August 1934.
13. *Ibid.*, 25 November 1937.

14. Charles W. Stokes in *The Advertising World*, vol. 63, No. 2.
15. Series of articles, *The Public and Football Pools, Daily Telegraph*, February 1938.
16. Brian V. Edsall in No. 14.
17. Aldous Huxley, *The Olive Tree*.
18. Quoted in A. S. J. Baster, *Advertising Reconsidered*.
19. In *Prose of Persuasion*.
20. *Middletown in Transition*.
21. *Patterns of Culture*.
22. M. Klein and J. Rivière, *Love, Hate and Reparation*.
23. *Daily Telegraph*, 26 May 1939.

CHAPTER IV

ADVERTISING AND THE PRESS

I. Dependence on advertising

To-day the newspaper is, in its commercial aspect as a matter of pounds, shillings and pence, a by-product of advertising.

THOMAS RUSSELL, *Commercial Advertising*

The influence of advertising is financially paramount: it goes deep and wide and permeates every line that is written and every picture published—yet its importance is most insufficiently appreciated. Not one in a thousand even of the twenty to thirty million readers of London newspapers owned and produced by the five chief financial groups is acutely and continually aware that what he reads is put before him in a manner, at a time and with reservations and omissions that are all subordinate to this main consideration.

JANE SOAMES, *The English Press*

TILL the time of Northcliffe, newspapers were generally regarded by their owners as public institutions, and policy was determined by the editor's idea of what was in the public interest. In spite of bitter partisanship and excessive pomposity this sense of responsibility was evident in their conduct, and there are instances of papers being run at a loss when the editor maintained views that ran counter to current opinion. Lord Northcliffe and his brother realised the possibilities of profit through advertising revenue, with the result that nowadays newspaper enterprise is a branch of commerce, with money or money power as the controlling motive. It has attracted financiers different from others only in that they are, or appear to be, more irresponsible and egoistic, and thus find in the Press a more suitable outlet for their talents than cement marketing. As Mr. Russell says, the newspaper is now a by-product of advertising. This is borne out by the fact that a typical two million sale daily will receive £1,800,000 a year from advertising, and £1,600,000 from sales (1).

II. Changes in the press—influence on news and policy

One consequence has been the concentration of newspaper control in the hands of very few men. Smaller papers have gone under, lacking the resources to advertise themselves and secure the circulation figures which attract a certain type of advertiser—though many have realised that it is the quality of a circulation, not the quantity, that counts. Before the war of 1914 there were six (and earlier eight) evening newspapers in London, four at 1d., two at ½d., the difference in price marking a sharp distinction in character; the halfpenny sheets were largely concerned with sport. After the war all the commercial advantage fell to those with the largest circulations, and now there are only three left, all working the same popular market. The *Daily Chronicle*, with nearly a million circulation, had to merge with the *Daily News* because it could not raise the advertising revenue required and could not keep pace with rising costs. (One insurance company demanded for free insurance schemes a deposit of £40,000 on a circulation of 200,000.) The *New Statesman and Nation* has incorporated three other journals of opinion. Finally, the *Morning Post*, as its biographer records, became 'in the incomparable words of an incomparable contemporary newspaper, a parasite in the advertising business'. Even the *Daily Worker* took to printing displayed advertisements.

The methods of advertising used by the Press, and the devices to secure circulation, cost immense sums. Express Newspapers spend £400,000 on advertising, and £100,000 on free insurance for readers, out of an income of £5,175,000 a year. According to the *Economist*, newspapers used to spend between one and three-quarters and two million pounds a year on canvassing; 'the evidence is conclusive that as soon as the canvassing effort of one newspaper ceases, the floating circulation which it has acquired drifts away to any other newspaper which may canvass the same ground.' (Lord Kemsley, Chairman of Allied Newspapers, Ltd.) The free sets of Dickens and other gifts are a comparatively recent memory, and it is worth recalling that when Lord Rothermere tried to float a newspaper in the Newcastle-on-Tyne district he gave away (according to the *Daily Telegraph*) free entertainment tickets and half-crown meals at the rate of £50,000 in six or eight weeks.

Most readers of periodicals will have noticed that their attention is frequently drawn to the advertisements by injunctions or articles which do not form part of the advertisements themselves. Thus in the same position on one of its more important pages the *Daily Mail* used regularly to print a little essay of 130 words or so, under some such caption as 'For Spring-Minded Men' with the conclusion:

> The nearness of spring is now reminding many a man that sunnier days will soon be revealing little shabbinesses previously unnoticed—and the advertisements appearing in the *Daily Mail* are equally reminding him of how men's outfitters and tailors are timely in their advance offers of colour and style in the new season's goods.

Or more glaring tie-ups such as this may be inserted among the reading matter:

NEWS IN THE ADVERTISING

Novelty Compact for the Home

Christmas Shopping will soon be in full swing. The search for novelties for the home has begun . . . [Attention was then drawn to several advertised items—condiments and a brand of magnesium hydroxide] (2).

The *News Chronicle* used to publish a series of articles under the general heading 'Aditorially', insisting on the merits of advertised goods as a whole. In one of these (19 August 1938), the Advertisement Director discussed branded goods, and the way in which people go on buying the same brand. 'It is just this fact which makes advertised goods so safe to buy. The manufacturer who has gone to the expense of persuading you to try his product is bound to give you value for money so that you may become a regular customer.' Among the numerous and attractive announcements which occupied other parts of the same day's issue there was a whole page advertisement for 'Vitamina'. Vitamina, 'the crystalline form of elements which plants and fruits extract from the soil and convert into vitalising Mineral Salts and Vitamins . . . completely rejuvenates the whole system and removes the "cause" of all nerve troubles.' Reinforced by several illustrated testimonials from titled people and others, it claimed remarkable results for many conditions, including rheumatism, blood pressure and all cases of nerves and debility. Other parts of the same issue contained advertisements for medicinal wine, stomach pills, small liver pills, obesity tablets and pain-killing pills.

An article in the *Daily Express*, while not formally directing attention to its advertisements, guarantees that all retail trade advertisements appearing in its columns contain no untrue or misleading statements. The *Daily Herald* (3) on the occasion of an Advertising Convention carried on its leader page a persuasively disinterested article on *The People's Purse* which remarked that 'the public now shows a marked preference for advertised goods, because they regard the advertisement itself as a guarantee'. With this type we are moving away from a direct invitation by the newspaper to notice specified goods, but a few cases should be noticed first. A journal devoted to a very popular hobby prints among its Editorial Topics a feature called *Do You Know*

A Weekly Series of questions for readers to test their knowledge of —————— *matters.* On turning to the answer page the reader is referred in every case to a section of three pages consisting entirely of write-ups of the products offered in advertisements. 'Write-ups' of course are the supporting articles, more or less paraphrases of the advertising matter, that the editor sometimes inserts because it is made a condition and he has no choice, or because he wishes to encourage advertisers. Cars, accessories, houses, travel, books, films are all written up in this way, the women's magazines being the most blatant offenders. One of the latter enclosed a postcard with every copy, listing thirty-four products or services of which the reader could get samples or leaflets on application to the journal.

Other methods used to develop the consumer's confidence are the reporting of every speech or publication that refers favourably to advertising and the insertion of advertisements of the Advertising Association. The tritest remark by a nobody quite unqualified to give an opinion will be placed in a favourable position by any popular daily if it says something nice about advertising, while more important events or speeches are omitted or compressed out of all proportion. The Conference of the Licensed Victuallers Defence League is not of striking interest to the layman, but if a speaker happens to mention that the success of Blackpool has been helped by advertising, the *Daily* —————— gives his remarks a quarter of a column. Nor would one have thought an article in the Manchester Chamber of Commerce monthly record to be of much concern to the readers of *The* ——, but because the subject is British Advertising the article gets a good summary in that paper (4). The Research and Publicity Department of the Advertising Association discovers that eighty prominent firms who one year made a profit of 38% or more are all professed believers in advertising; the daily papers wrote this up as something that mattered and listed most of the firms. And so with the dinners of the Institute of Incorporated Practitioners in Advertising, the meetings of a Management Conference, the luncheons of the Publicity Club. But the meetings or the article or the books which present something new or vital, will be neglected —or distorted, if they can be given some 'human interest' twist.

In recent years the Advertising Association, and perhaps other bodies, have been responsible for the use in the London and provincial Press of a good deal of space to advertise advertising. Under the heading 'How Advertising Protects the Public' a few well-spaced paragraphs explain why 'there is safety in a branded name'. Another is entitled 'There's only Good News in the advertisements', while a third enjoins us to 'Read the advertisements and keep up-to-date'. A more ambitious type has a pen drawn bird's-eye view of what looks like a board of directors meeting in a salon; and beneath, headed *Family Finance*, followed this piece:

> Do they realise how quickly children's shoes wear out; that new babies cost money; that stair-carpet does not last for ever; that a fellow likes to take his wife out on Saturday night . . . that folks are *human*?
>
> The honest truth is that most mothers . . . have to be certain that everything they buy is the best value they can get.
>
> Isn't it natural then that they rely on those goods which they see advertised in this paper over and over again? These are the goods with a name to keep up; with a reputation to maintain!

There are in addition various unseen pressures upon editors to publish news items or editorial matter favourable to advertisers, though the convention that no brand names are mentioned in editorial columns is carefully observed, because it would be impossible to please all advertisers this way. The convention is carried to comic lengths when well-known firms or products have to be formally camouflaged, and the Ministry of Food has to call Marmite 'a vegetable extract' in its recipes.

My first example of how attempts are made to influence editorial policy is classical. It is quoted from the *Observer* and the speaker was Sir Edgar Sanders, a director of the Brewers' Society.

> While I do not wish to say anything disrespectful of the Press, I know that they had some idea that we were contemplating a large advertising scheme if we got a reduction in the beer duty, as the Press, particularly the commercial side, came and asked me all sorts of questions about this. I said that first we had to get a reduction in the duty, and I think there is no doubt whatever that this had some effect, because the commercial side are always pestering the editorial side. In the same way, if we begin advertising in the Press, we shall see that the continuation of our advertising is contingent upon the fact that we get editorial support as well in the same papers. In that way it is wonderful how you can educate public opinion, generally without making it too obvious that there is a publicity campaign behind it all.

I am glad to say that this attempt met with great opposition, and failed.

Such cases rarely come out, and this one may not be typical. There is probably nothing in England to parallel the way in which the American power and lighting utilities made use of the newspapers for covert propaganda (cf. F. E. Lumley, *The Propaganda Menace*). Here is another instance. Readers may remember that a certain London daily occasionally runs campaigns against the Co-operative Societies, explicitly in defence of 'the small man'. According to *The Week* (5) one of the motives of this campaign was as follows: it had been reported that the 'Co-op' were proposing to set up a big store in the west end of London. This alarmed a well-known Oxford Street department store, a large advertiser in the newspaper concerned. If the Co-ops had their

way, the profits of the department store, and hence indirectly of the paper, would be diminished.

A more recent example of successful interference with
editorial policy comes from the early days of the present
war when all sections of the Press boasted of our not having
to ration. According to the *Political Quarterly* (6) 'this
attitude was fostered by certain groups of trades and advertisers who used the national Press to carry on a violent anti-
rationing campaign. According to a statement by Mr. A. V.
Alexander, which was never officially denied, the Cabinet
yielded to pressure and vetoed rationing, though the Ministry
of Food was prepared to introduce a scheme within a month
of the outbreak of war.' In January 1940 *The Times* gave
the leading position in its correspondence to a long letter
from the Champagne Association and the Bordeaux Agents'
Association. They argued that the Government economy
propaganda was mistaken in calling 'upon every section of
the community drastically to cut down the consumption of
all luxury articles'. Before Christmas 1939, advertisements
had appeared in many papers inviting us to drink French
wines; the campaign is said to have cost £28,000. Even in
1941 the protests of the cosmetic trade against the limitation
of supplies to 25% succeeded in obtaining editorial support
(7). We realise now that the chief fault of rationing and non-
spending schemes was the fact that they were applied years
too late; and that the efforts of advertisers to determine
policy were short-sighted and against the national interest.
It may even have endangered our food supply. Speaking on
2 September 1941, the Parliamentary Secretary to the
Ministry of Food said that at one stage of the war food
imports were at a dangerously low level.

With the intention of pleasing their advertisers, newspapers, if they do not actually invent news, exaggerate the
importance of small items to such an extent that invention is
the impression left. Are the readers of a national newspaper

really interested in the fact that the 'Ovaltine' Jersey Herd took three firsts at the Wallingford Show? (8). Or that the Quins, with the aid of Quaker Oats nerve-nourishing Vitamin B, 'guard against indigestion, poor appetite and nerviness due to lack of the vitamin'? (8). A newspaper may promote or, shall we say, develop a potential news-item. The Campbell-Black flight to Australia, for instance, must have brought in a good access of advertising revenue; the airmen carried, or gave testimonials for, some thirty kinds of food, material and clothing—there may have been more. This kind of news has increased since the Public Relations Officers of institutions such as the Post Office as well as of private enterprises have found that an effective way of securing free publicity is to set going the works for some event which will have news and hence advertising value. Even a reduction in the price of a car has been the occasion for a paragraph in the *Daily* ――― (9), and the same organ gave a column of its space to an account, doubtless of some news value, of how two Morris cars, an old and a new, were collided, in order to prove the superiority of new methods of construction (10).

The supply of news by publicity organisations and Press agents was defended by Mr. J. E. Williams in the *Spectator* (11):

> Real hard industrial news should play an increasingly important part in newspapers. Such news helps the industries concerned by the publicity it gives them, and, therefore, helps the prosperity of the country in general. . . . The practice of issuing synthetic news is certainly to be deplored, but surely any editor can distinguish it from the genuine article.

But, one must ask, will the Advertising Manager let him? Another view of synthetic news is that of Mr. Montgomery Belgion (12):

> The aim . . . is to make the public conscious of—to imagine some examples—a railway company, an alcoholic beverage, a night club, a process of avoiding infection with tuberculosis, or

a trade union, by causing the public to notice *almost unawares* the railway company's enterprise, the ancient customs observed in connection with the beverage, the fashionable people who patronise the night club, a celebrity's support of the process of avoiding infection with tuberculosis, or the trade union's entertainment of a distinguished former member. That is to say, the aim is to put the emphasis on something else and to make the public conscious of a concern, an article of consumption, or a movement, surreptitiously. . . . The result is that the public is being subjected to a vast amount of insidious suggestion.

Complementary to the invention of synthetic news and the insertion of articles favourable to advertisers is the suppression of news and views that would displease or injure them. Till the war reduced the amount of advertising space in the Press, it was impossible to find anything unfavourable to Patent Medicines; though when in July 1941 the Pharmacy and Medicines Bill was read a second time, some papers, notably the *Daily Telegraph*, gave a very fair summary of the debate in which patent medicines were denounced at length. At one time a daily newspaper, which ran a series of stunts to stimulate sales, helped to circulate the theme 'The whiter the bread, the sooner you're dead'. But after the processers of flour united to promote the sale of bread by advertising, nothing against white bread ever appeared. And the following notice appeared in a national newspaper office:

MEMO TO SUB-EDITORS

Don't pass anything detrimental to BREAD. To say that bread is fattening, for instance, is detrimental (13).

Another example of suppression was exposed by Dr. Edith Summerskill speaking in the House of Commons, 18 July 1940:

I have crusaded against this unsafe milk supply for years. What surprises me is that the Government know it. I think that eighteen months ago the then Minister of Agriculture

K

threatened to introduce a Milk Bill in this House, and that one of the provisions was that the milk supplied to the community should all be pasteurised. Then pressure was brought to bear upon the Government by the vested interests throughout the country, the vested interests who are fattening upon the unholy profits made out of the sale of tubercular-infected milk, vested interests so strong that what I am saying will never appear in any newspaper in the country because the advertisements might cease if the milk was not sold (14).

The following evidence is also relevant, though strictly it does not come under the heading Suppression of News. In January 1938 the British Medical Association, in order to warn the public against the risk of drinking milk which is neither tuberculin-tested nor pasteurised, prepared an announcement and offered it to many leading periodicals. The advertisements, which explained the risk by citing a number of facts about deaths caused by infected milk, duly appeared in some provincial dailies and weekly reviews, but the advertisement managers of the national dailies refused to accept it. The Newspaper Proprietors' Association, suffering from a unique rush of virtue to the head, eventually gave as its reasons that the arguments and examples were misleading, that the advertisement was prejudicial to the national milk campaign (incidentally a leading advertiser) and that it represented a use of 'scare' methods which might be discounted by the public in a commercial advertiser, but was an objectionable technique for use by a body like the B.M.A. (15). Eventually the copy was slightly changed and appeared in all national papers except the *Daily Express*.

From America comes an instance of the suppression of news in the interests of advertisers. During the Chicago World Fair there was an epidemic of amœbic dysentery, which was entirely suppressed by the Chicago newspapers, because the news would have reduced the income of big advertisers such as hotels and department stores.

There are plenty of other cases of newspapers refusing to accept advertisements. Major van der Byl, who carries on propaganda against methods of obtaining fur which sound cruel to an incredible degree, says that 'only very few papers now have the courage to print letters exposing the cruelties of the fur trade, and my advertisements have been refused owing to complaints by the fur advertisers.' In America, businesses about which newspapers are never permitted to make unfavourable comment are known as 'sacred cows'. One such beast, particularly nutritious to the British Press because it used to pay £3,000,000 a year in advertising, is the patent medicine trade. How this trade has influenced the Press is shown by this quotation (para. 28) from the Report of the Select Committee of 1914 on Patent and Proprietary Medicines:

> We must point out . . . that the large sums received for the advertisement of secret remedies lead newspapers, either from discretion or under compulsion, to exclude from their columns criticism or discussion of secret remedies. When the British Medical Association, for example, issued their volume entitled 'Secret Remedies', containing analyses, costs, etc., of a large number of proprietary medicines, not only was the volume not noticed editorially by most papers, but even an advertisement of it was declined by many journals, some of the highest class. A trial in Edinburgh in the course of which the judge described the business of the proprietors of '—— ——' as 'based on unblushing falsehood for the purpose of defrauding the public' was, we were informed, with few exceptions not reported in the Press, and the remedy still has a considerable sale.

In his short book on *Patent Medicines*, Prof. A. J. Clark pointed out that the makers of patent medicines control the Press, and the Press controls the politicians. 'The most interesting feature of the influence exerted by the trade in proprietary medicines directly on the Press and indirectly

on the House of Commons is the comparative smallness of
the trade which exerts this influence. . . . Its peculiarity is
that, because it is selling rubbish at high prices, it has a very
big margin to spare for advertisement. Hence the political
influence it can exert is out of all proportion to its magnitude.' The occasional glimpses one gets of advertisement
pressure at work makes one suspect that the choice of matter
in periodicals is considerably determined by the direct or
indirect influence of advertisers. From America a case is
reported where an article on making soup was banned from
a woman's magazine because this would increase intelligent
dieting among housewives and decrease the sale of tinned
foods.

Financial advertisements, especially in the form of reports
of company meetings, bring in a good deal of revenue to
daily, Sunday and weekly papers, and are the mainstay of
financial newspapers. Strong pressure is brought to bear on
financial editors to give favourable notice to prospectuses
for new issues of shares (16). It is safe to say that prospectuses rarely meet with thorough or impartial criticism; newspapers are profit-making concerns, and are naturally reluc-
tant to bring too strong a light to play on the affairs of other
money-making enterprises. Mr. A. S. J. Baster, in *Advertising Reconsidered*, surmises that the damage done during
the pre-1929 period of boom finance could have been prevented by a free and outspoken financial Press. There is no
doubt that during the same period in the U.S.A. similar
damage was caused by silence on the part of the Press. 'It
was distinctly bad business to offend utility companies,
Florida real-estate promoters, and investment banking
houses, and thus to run the risk of losing highly remunerative
advertising . . . there was hardly any critical examination of,
let us say, the Insull holding-company pyramid in the days
when it was being built to the skies; there was hardly a voice
raised against the excesses of the Florida real-estate boom in

1925 or of the stock-market boom in 1928 and 1929—until after they had crashed' (17).

Before this section is closed, one point should be cleared up. The action of advertisement managers in refusing the B.M.A. warning against unsafe milk may have surprised some readers who imagined that the advertising columns of the newspapers are, like justice, free to all those who can afford to pay up. That, of course, is not so. The Newspaper Proprietors' Association has agreed with its members that they will not publish in the papers any advertisements which criticise or attack products advertised in their columns. Some provincial newspapers have refused to accept advertisements for temperance meetings because the announcement of the meeting contained some reference to its object, and in 1938 the *Observer* refused an advertisement of a book called *Behind the Spanish Barricades* which supported the Republican side in the Civil War. The newspapers insist on the right to refuse or amend advertising in order to keep within the law—they would be liable if any advertisement were libellous or seditious—and especially to avoid 'knocking' advertisements, i.e. those which run down competing products. To the consumer it might seem healthy that competitors should thus state their own claims and have them weighed by others—rather more of the truth would appear. But such rivalry would naturally discredit advertising as such in the eyes of the public, and the inclusive claims made for its reliability would be weakened; that is what the Advertising Managers do not want, hence the ban on 'knocking' advertisements. Actually a good many border-line cases do seem to get passed; even if the indication of a rival is no preciser than 'Refuse all Imitations' it is often easy to identify the competitor in question. In particular the vendors of remedies for constipation do not hesitate to depreciate other medicines or types of relief. Nor do the newspapers themselves keep strictly to the principle behind the N.P.A.

agreement, in that they will themselves deliver vigorous attacks (not necessarily frontal) upon other media of advertising, of which they are naturally very jealous. The *Observer*, for instance, published an article in a prominent position: 'Reduce Posters by Half—An Expert's Advice', and the same paper has often had articles, excellent in themselves, about the destruction of rural amenities by posters and crude catering signs, at the same time opening its correspondence columns to letters propagating the point of view of the C.P.R.E. and making even more spirited attacks upon the interests involved. On 5 January 1938, the *Daily Telegraph* could find no confirmation for reports that the French Government had agreed to ban the broadcasting of advertising in English by French radio stations, 'though it is admitted that the question has been under consideration for some time as the result of representations from Great Britain.' Later, Mr. Eden, in answer to a question in the House, admitted that he had asked the French Government to suppress sponsored programmes in English from stations in France. It was suggested that this action was taken at the instance of certain newspapers, and the way in which a popular newspaper reported the ban confirms the suggestion, for in its issue of February 8th it disingenuously attempted to class commercial broadcasts with the political propaganda put out by Bari.

III. Synthetic optimism

So far we have given instances of advertising pressure on behalf of particular products or interests. But there is another way in which the choice of news and the character of the commentary on the news are affected by advertising. Its nature is suggested by a comment of Sir Frank Newnes at the 42nd annual general meeting of George Newnes, Ltd.

'The reduction in the profits was caused by the increase in the cost of paper and the lower advertisement revenues of some of the company's publications due to the unsettling effect of the international situation.' This is only one of many like observations made at company meetings, disclosing that crises such as the Abdication, the Abyssinian War, the Spanish Civil War, Munich, and in fact any period when the interest of the public is more deeply engaged in serious topics or international affairs, cause the public's willingness to spend to dry up, and make advertising unprofitable. People will not spend in an apprehensive mood, and the newspapers therefore must try to produce a mood of optimism, whether the facts justify it or not.

This manufactured optimism runs throughout every column of a popular paper—in the 'slant' put on the news, in the playing down or omission of news which might be depressing, in the editorials, the comic strips, the smiling faces in the advertisements and the picture page. Mr. H. N. Brailsford speaks with authority as a leader-writer and ex-editor (what he says of advanced papers, in *Property or Peace*, applies to the whole Press):

> Advanced papers are subject, as it were, to a continued censorship by an invisible censor, who can ruin the enterprise. ... There is thus a continuous pressure towards moderation and understatement. Dangerous topics are tabooed, a campaign boldly begun is inexplicably dropped, risky bits of news find their way to the wastepaper basket, or to the smallest type on a back page. The shadow of the advertiser broods ... throughout the office, presiding ... over the selection of topics for editorial comment, and above all over the selection of news. The trend is always towards safety; radical turns liberal and socialist fades to labour.

The drive towards an optimism that will distract the attention of readers from the worries of their own lives and the complications of international affairs affects even the reports of foreign correspondents stationed thousands of miles away. Foreign correspondents of the professional kind are intelligent men, alive to their responsibilities. It is important work, because it determines the impression of the government and policy of foreign countries that the public at home receives. On these impressions the public votes for the proponents of one or another foreign policy, and in this way matters of co-operation between nation and nation, issues that tip the balance between war and peace, are decided. But rarely can the foreign correspondent send the reports that his conscience and sense of responsibility dictate—or if he sends them, they will be neglected or hopelessly distorted. An instance of the latter is brought to mind by reading in the papers (September 1941) that Britain is requesting Turkey to carry out one of the provisions of the Treaty of Montreux. I remember that while the *Eastern Daily Press* gave a full version of the original discussions that led up to the Treaty and reported virtual agreement among the delegates, the *Daily Mail* on the same day reported 'complete deadlock on most of the vital questions' and went on to give an account of how the delegates visited the famous 'Castle of Chillon immortalised by Byron's poem, while Swiss girls made merry round a maypole'. In order to keep up the circulation on which revenue is gained, the editors of popular papers insistently demand speed in the despatch of reports and 'human interest' in their content. When serious papers were asking for interpretations of political events in Rumania, one London editor demanded a 'description of Madame Lupescu's boudoir, for to-morrow'. The Vienna correspondent could not contact Bucharest, but a description was despatched from Vienna two hours later (18).

So in the years before 1939, when this country was drifting into war, the public was persistently non-informed about foreign affairs, and it chose its leaders and policy accordingly. In his *Georgian Adventure*, Mr. Douglas Jerrold, apropos of the fact that advertisers don't like newspapers with views, has related how he wrote to Lord Beaverbrook, who understood that the late 1936 version of Government foreign policy meant war, inevitably, to suggest that his readers should be told regularly what was happening abroad. Lord Beaverbrook wrote a charming letter but the editor 'informed me that the *Daily Express* had no space for such a feature as I suggested. No space. The issue, on Lord Beaverbrook's own premisses, is one of life and death for the whole of Europe. No space? These are the mathematics of Bedlam.' It is not necessary to hold Mr. Jerrold's political views to see the point that any serious discussion of international affairs was debarred by a section of the Press.

Accordingly the drift continued and the newspapers, whose advertisers had suffered from loss of trade during the crisis, were proclaiming that the country was solidly pro-Chamberlain and that permanent peace was on the way. Perhaps this attitude was not unconnected with the announcement by Mr. E. W. White, managing director of the Star Advertising Company, that

> I have been appointed by a group of members of the House of Commons to undertake a campaign on behalf of certain members of the House of Commons to establish Neville Chamberlain in the position he has taken up regarding his foreign policy and also to back him up against his detractors (19).

After Munich, on Sunday, 9 October 1938, Hitler told Great Britain to mind her own business and placed his veto on the return to office of three prominent British politicians. The news was broadcast in the evening, but on the Monday morning some of the leading papers were almost apologetic. Then (in the words of Mr. Wickham Steed, *The Press*, p. 249) 'Enquiry into this humiliating behaviour on the part of our "free Press" elicited the information that certain large advertising agents had warned journals for which they provide much revenue that advertisements would be withheld from them should they "play up" the international crisis and cause an alarm which was "bad for trade". None of the newspapers thus warned dared to publish the names of these advertisement agents or to hold them up to public contempt. And this at a moment when it is of the utmost national importance to unite the country in defence of its freedom and, maybe, of its independent existence.' In the House of Commons the accusation was repeated, but it was denied by Sir William Crawford at the annual dinner of the Institute of Incorporated Practitioners in Advertising, reported in the *Daily Telegraph* for 16 December 1938.

Still, the *Daily Express* went on proclaiming 'There will be no war', and as late as early in 1939 the late Lord Rothermere was saying that Hitler was a great gentleman. And the war started. The reader may be interested at this point in the explanation of Mr. W. E. Tomlin, advertising manager of the *News Chronicle*:

> As I was one of those who continued to preach optimism when the Crisis first began to look serious, I think I have a right to remind advertisers once more that there is plenty of room for development in this country. . . . I am, of course, quite well aware that confidence is the one thing which is supremely necessary for the expansion to begin. But confidence is in many ways synonymous with courage and no advertiser has ever succeeded without a generous measure of that quality (20).

A possible indirect influence upon the Press is the expenditure by Government departments of large sums on advertising space. From September 1939 to June 1942 inclusive, departments spent a total of £3,805,000 on Press advertising, apart from posters (21). (In peace time approximately nine times as much is spent on Press as on Poster advertising.) The largest items came from the Ministry of Food (£855,000), then National Savings (£1,251,100) and the Air Ministry (£414,000). In war time, of course, the Government has more than sufficient control over the Press in all issues affecting national security; but it is easy to imagine that in peace time, and in war time when a paper's attitude towards the politicians in power for the time being is not complaisant, Government departments could bring pressure to bear on newspapers simply by withholding advertisements and granting inadequate facilities for attending conferences and collecting news. In an article on 'Government Advertising' Dr. W. A. Robson gave some instances:

> How many people realise the enormous influence of advertisements on the attitude of newspapers towards departmental policy? For several months of the war a number of national newspapers ran persistent campaigns attacking the Ministry of Food. The Ministry began to buy advertising space on a large scale and the attacks mysteriously disappeared. The Ministry of Transport was violently criticised for the heavy toll of road accidents caused by the black-out. The Ministry began to appeal to the public to take greater care in costly advertisements, and no more was heard of its sins.

IV. The freedom of the press?

It will be seen from the evidence given that the 'freedom of the Press' is very considerably qualified. However independent and responsible an editor may be himself, he does not decide the emphasis that shall be placed on news or the interpretation of the news given in articles and editorials. An important member of the staff of a national newspaper reported to a Mass-observer: 'I've had my Advertising Manager coming in every day and telling me, "Look here, old boy, you can't possibly put that in, it'll scare off our advertisers."' The influence of the Advertising Manager is paramount; in fact he is sometimes the highest-paid member of the staff. Even the whims of the proprietor are subordinate, as when the vigorous support given to the Fascist movement by one of Lord ————'s papers was throttled by the advertising department.

There is no doubt that over whole tracts of social life, politics and economics we do not get information or interpretation from the Press. It is rather in the accumulation of small suppressions, a daily misplacing of stress than in any deliberate programme, that we find the influence of advertising. For example, when the Duke of Windsor, as Prince of Wales, insisted while visiting Vienna on seeing the magnificent blocks of flats put up by the socialist municipality of the city, his interest and tour of inspection were simply neglected by popular papers, which preferred to give pictures of the Prince at a cabaret. In the same way when he visited distressed areas of S. Wales, he was shocked at what he saw and observed that they should import a few Viennese plans. The suppression of such items may or may not have something to do with the fact that papers derive a large income from building societies, house agents and a large section of private owners using the classified advertisements which in peace time account for about half the advertising space in *The Times* and *Telegraph*. These people would not have welcomed any enquiry into the profits of agents and owners, or a programme of rehousing and State acquisition. In the same way the facts which the B.M.A. wished to present to the public in the interest of the public should have been made available by the Press; and if it had not been so serious it would have been comic to find the N.P.A. taking a high moral line about the B.M.A. advertisement when at the same moment their news-sheets were carrying the intimidating or wheedling solicitations of such public benefactors as the patent medicine vendors. As the PEP Report notes, under the heading *Neglect of Consumer Interests*, 'It is especially remarkable that although all readers are consumers, anything touching the interests of consumers as a whole, such as the high cost of distributing certain commodities, is apt to be given little prominence. . . . It is particularly in the sphere of health education that advertising interests—baby foods, patent medicines, dentifrices, tobacco, intoxicating liquors, white bread, meat extracts—embarrass and hamper the Press in performing a function which would be a real national benefit.'

Mention should also be made of the relations between advertising and periodicals other than the national papers. Some of the excellent provincial papers, being unable to produce impressive circulations, are unable to attract much revenue from national advertisers, and find it difficult to pay their way. It is said of one or two that they live on the profits of evening newspapers working at a much lower level of appeal. On the other hand I have heard it said that one provincial paper had such a local demand for space that it could afford to neglect the national advertisers. The need to live by advertising revenue is especially inimical to papers of 'advanced' or left or liberal views; few can show circulations of any magnitude and advertisers are afraid of them. This squeezing-out of independent periodicals is deplorable; in the past they have been a normal source of sap for the intellectual life of the country, and their influence has spread far beyond their actual purchasers. The views and the standards they set were quoted and respected; they acted as schools for young and intelligent journalists. The effect of advertising on specialist, technical, medical and literary publications is discussed under other headings.

The worst side of the influence of advertising on the Press is not deception, the control of buying habits, the subsidising of dictator-minded owners by what is in effect a tax on food, lingerie, toilet and 'consumption' goods generally, or the inculcation of anti-social policies, but the development of a new type of newspaper, and one which may have fatal results for the democracy it thrives on. For all its superb technical equipment, its marvellously efficient organisation for collecting news, the intelligence of some of its editors and many of its writers, the modern popular Press cannot be said to represent Progress. Progress in some spheres we know as a fact; we can get from London to Edinburgh with greater speed and more comfort than before; when the electricity fails we put in a new fuse or call in an electrician instead of offering sacrifices to the fire-god. But we still conduct some of our affairs at this primitive level. The Press must have advertising revenue; the advertisers think they must have big circulations; the Press controllers seem to find it necessary to cater for the lowest common factors in the public to get these circulations. So instead of using what might be called 'scientific' means of informing the public so that it will choose 'scientific' methods of managing its affairs, and rulers who will put to social uses the great resources of science, we find that in the presentation of news and views 'the present almost exclusive reliance upon the anecdotal method is fed by the proprietor's desire to be exciting in order to sell copies in order to raise advertising revenue' (23). We allow relatively unimportant and irresponsible sections of industry to inculcate trivial interests and undesirable habits of mind.

The reader's sense of proportion, of what matters to him and what can be left to others, his scales of value, are affected by the ratio of space given to various activities by the Press. Sport has taken more and more space, partly because it is one of the distractions that it pays the Press to offer, partly because sport in this century has become a business, with expensive accessories to be advertised, commercial football clubs providing a staple of 'news', and opulent pools and betting firms who will buy space. In peace *The Times* always had a 'solus' advertisement on the sports page, which was sought after by advertisers (at the rate of £77 an issue for space amounting to a column), presumably because the reader is in a plastic, receptive, taking-it-easy state of mind when he reads the sports news. Again I do not think it is exaggerating to say that the mere fact that advertisements occupy a great deal of space arranges our scale of proportion for us; we come to feel that because advertised goods and services take up half or more of our daily paper they should engage half of our time and interest. This is serious in peace time, if I am right; it matters even more in war time, for apart from accounting for 60,000 tons of shipping space in paper a year, advertising may squeeze out of our four- or six-page dailies articles giving us the background and interpretation of the news, or the reports of Parliamentary debates. A wider public acquaintance with these reports seems particularly vital to the war effort and the maintenance of civil liberties.

REFERENCES TO CHAPTER IV

1. *Economist*, 7 January 1937.
2. *Reynolds News*, 14 November 1937.
3. 19 June 1939.
4. 28 September 1933.
5. No. 45.
6. July–September 1941, p. 261.
7. *Economist*, 15 February 1941.
8. *Reynolds News*, 22 May 1938.
9. 20 January 1939.
10. 11 May 1939.
11. 3 February 1939.
12. *Fortnightly Review*, March 1938.
13. PEP *Report on the Press*, p. 197.
14. *Official Report*, House of Commons, column 515.
15. No. 13, p. 183.
16. No. 13 has a good account on p. 198.

17. F. L. Allen, *Lords of Creation*, p. 230.
18. 'Robert Powell' writing on 'The Foreign Correspondent', *Fortnightly Review*, February 1941.
19. *Spectator*, 7 October 1938.
20. Mass-Observation Penguin, *Britain*.
21. *Official Report*, House of Commons, 23 July 1942.
22. *Political Quarterly*, July-September 1940.
23. H. D. Lasswell, *World Politics and Personal Insecurity*.

CHAPTER V

WHAT CAN BE DONE WITH ADVERTISING?

I. In the post-war economy

IN conversation one occasionally hears advertisers attacked or derided. But such views rarely appear in print because the state of the libel laws and the nature of the Press prevent open criticism. Various opinion-testing agencies have taken the views of what some people think about certain advertisements, but not what they feel about advertising; and to judge by the success of much advertising, it operates without the victim knowing much about it. The only occasion on which the views of the public—or a small selected sample of it— have been made known was when the late *Week-end Review* (1) asked its readers to reply to a questionnaire. 835 people gave their verdict, and it was a severe one. In the main they supported the conclusion, reached by the writer of a series of articles on advertising in the same journal, that 'the excessive volume and over-competitive nature (of advertising) spring from a faulty and basically unsound structure of distribution . . . not self-contained evils to be attacked in themselves, but represent a distributive organisation that is due for thorough overhauling and a social atmosphere that is unhealthy to a quite unnecessary extent.'

If an economic system of production for use rather than for profit could be achieved, the worst features of advertising would be removed. The U.S.S.R. is an example of a country which adopts twentieth-century manufacturing technique without twentieth-century sales talk. There the State is producer and distributor. The bigger Soviet stores, for instance, are said to have none of the eye-catching luxury features of Western shops, showcases and 'service' accessories—post-office, writing- and rest-rooms. Nor are they adorned with commissionaires, page-boys and lift-girls, which give the Westerner the air of luxury he is supposed to like. According to Mr. Huntly Carter, 'the elaborate foreign system of selling by household canvass with its many evils is practically unknown. There is practically no system of stimulation of sales by the use of persuasion or pressure. On the pictorial or display side of the store there may be a little persuasion.' According to the Webbs, however, advertising of a kind does exist, the difference being in the way whereby the changes of taste or fashion, caused in Europe by heavy advertisers, are brought about. 'In the Soviet Union the various scientific institutes, together with other research organisations directly connected with producing trusts or government departments, or with the consumers' co-operative movement, are constantly at work upon discovering what is the most advantageous consumption' (2). They study the nutrition value of foods, the functions of vitamins; the hygienic effects of different textiles and building materials; diet, work and recreation. This work seldom results in legal prescription, but is made the subject of intense popular propaganda.

It is unnecessary to demonstrate at length that before 1939 we had in this country 'a faulty and basically unsound system of distribution'. But it is worth presenting a few facts taken from *The Home Market* (rev. ed.), a publication which is a by-product of advertising. Just before the war, 0·3% of all persons of twenty-five years of age and over possessed 42% of all wealth in the country, or an average of £93,000 each; the remaining 99·7% possessed 58%, or an average of £375 each. Figures for the distribution of the national income bring out a more striking inequality. Two-thirds of all incomes were below £3 per week and amounted to two-fifths of the national income, while 3·1% of all income receivers (those above £500 a year) enjoyed 22·4 of the national income. It is the figure for two-thirds of all incomes that is of interest. It seems odd that £150,000,000 a year should be spent in persuading people to buy what they do not need, ought not to want or cannot afford, when the greater proportion of the population is living at or below subsistence level.

This is not the place to suggest in detail how the country should be run after the war. But a few considerations of what the country is likely to need for years after the war may be recorded. We find in war time that we are living reasonably well on mainly rationed and unadvertised foods; clothing and housing—we get what we can, advertised or not; and where luxury goods, say cigarettes, are concerned, we are glad to buy any supplies we can, irrespective of brand or advertisement. We have seen advertising of the persuasive kind greatly decrease in our newspapers; and it is not easy to see why any advertising should return, except the genuinely informative and desirable kind. If the present healthy clearing is to continue, there will be a much better chance for informative advertising, and the medium as a whole may recover some of the credit that it has lost through abuse.

Buildings and their accessories are what we shall need after the war. Rolling stock and repairs to stations and permanent way. New motor vehicles and intelligently planned roads. To take housing: on the basis of the figures for bomb damage to buildings given by Lord Keynes in January 1941, the equivalent of 500,000 houses will have to be built for every year of aerial war. In addition to this it has been calculated (4) that arrears in slum clearance and abatement of overcrowding would amount to 440,000 dwellings over the period of a three-years war. The broadsheet adds that owing to the likely gradual increase for some time in the number of families, 290,000 new dwellings will be needed, and concludes that 'it will probably be necessary to build well over one million houses for every year during which bombing continues'. In addition, many public and industrial buildings will be required. 2,000,000 houses means 50,000,000,000 bricks, 7,000,000 tons of cement, and 3,750,000 tons of coal to produce the cement. Then there will be a need for grates and baths and fittings for the new houses; and even in the undamaged homes there will be a huge demand for such things as radios, hollow-ware, crockery. After the war the money will be there; the goods won't. Advertising will be superfluous, to say the least.

What is happening during the war is that the usual relations of supply and demand have been inverted. The demand for most products outstrips the supply, and the need, if ever there was one, for persuasive advertising has vanished. The change in some ways has been salutary, and we need to retain the elements of health that have been forcibly thrust upon us. Are we to go back to the over-eating of meat that prevailed, among those who could afford it, in peace time? Are we to develop the growing of English apples of a flavour unexcelled—or are we to revert to the imported mass products of waxy appearance and soapy texture that display so well? Or to take the demand for radios; are the wireless firms, which are now doing war work, to compete in cramming sets on to the market and crowding on all the sales pressure they can, or will they compare notes before going into production, and seriously try to hand on the benefits of mass-production? If designs were shared, components could be mass-produced much more cheaply and repairs would be facilitated; one firm might concentrate on miniature radios, another on radiograms, another on 'freak' or luxury sets, another on sets specially designed for musical fidelity. And they might find out where the greatest demands would be, so that a maker in the midlands would not be supplying London, and a firm on the Great West Road would not be sending his sets to the North-East. These are, of course, random suggestions and it would be a delusion to imagine that they could be put into practice under our present economic system. They point to a need for less competition, more examination from a social point of view of what sales should or should not be promoted.

One war-time claim specially made for advertising deserves to be considered. We shall find, after the war, that if we consider it desirable to return to our pre-1939 material standard of living, depending on many imported goods, a large increase in exports will be needed. If this is possible, and it may not be, because so many dominions[1] and countries are now making for themselves what we used to supply them with, there may be some ground for the argument (put forward in the Advertising Association's leaflet *The Function of Advertising in War-time*) that in order to secure markets after, and to preserve 'good-will' during the war, there is a 'case for carefully written advertisements in the foreign Press and in papers with effective circulation oversea'. There is a case, if we are to assume that a return is to be made to the good old days of unrestricted competition between nations. Whether that is desirable or not, we need not discuss. Whether the return is effected or not depends on the relations between this country and the U.S.A.

But when the immediate post-war problems have been solved, what sort of a future is there for advertising? We may assume that there cannot be a return to pre-1939 conditions. The exact shape of things cannot be foreseen, but either the form of monopoly capitalism developed during the war will retain its grip—in which case we may expect a good deal of persuasive advertising to be used to make us buy the goods and services we would not otherwise have purchased, and to maintain between components of a monopoly the shadow-competition which appears to be effective in forcing up demand; or an economy may be adopted where staple demands are impartially assessed and

---

[1] e.g. the market for English light bulbs was even before the war considerably curtailed by the making of bulbs in Eire and Australia.

satisfied as well as can be, while 'floating' demands are controlled through advertising by qualified representatives of society.

Monopoly capitalism appears to be a form of dictatorship conducted on behalf of the dictators. But if eventually we get another form of government it will have a view of the ordinary man different from that held by commercial interest and many politicians—the view, roughly speaking, that man is a collection of mainly animal impulses, concerned only to make enough money to satisfy them. That seems to be the real view behind many advertisements. It is not a very flattering picture of humanity, but the constant upholding of and working on this view tends to make it a truer one than it was before advertising started. On the surface, however, advertising professes to believe that the consumer is qualified to assess the claims of competing products and capable of choosing for himself between the possibilities put before him, advertised or not. The directors of the good society will not assume that the ordinary man is thus omnicompetent—he plainly isn't—nor will they take it for granted that man is moved entirely by economic or material motives. We have seen a society in which a well-to-do suburban section has had most of the satisfactions deemed desirable by advertising, but spiritually and intellectually dead, lacking any common or individual purpose in life. At the same time a large number of people have been without an adequate wage, sufficient rest or security, and have therefore been special victims of the predatory advertiser. What Serge Chakotin wrote of propaganda applies equally well here: 'An overworked or ailing or hungry man with his nervous system upset or weakened, will succumb relatively easily to the force of suggestion. Thus eubiotics, the improvement of the conditions of existence . . . will quickly consolidate popular resistance to the enemy forces aiming at the physical and psychical enslavement of the people' (4).

To ensure such economic security, it will be necessary to co-ordinate production and consumption both within nations, by such means as the U.S.S.R. is described as using, and internationally, by commodity controls. Such an equilibrium has been difficult to attain because of the impossibility of predicting changes in public taste, or perhaps because there has been no co-ordination between the many would-be manipulators of the public mind. It will mean that the consumer will not have the absolutely free choice which is his, according to the advocates of advertising—a free choice which where existent can be carried to fantastic lengths; in 1937 a single London store—Selfridges—offered 10,763 kinds of stockings and 135 tooth pastes (5). It is here that Sir Richard Acland in his *What it will be like* and Karl Mannheim see a use for some advertising techniques. The latter suggests that

> In a democratic society this reduction in the incalculable variety of future consumption . . . might be attained by means of an advertising campaign, provided that it was carefully co-ordinated with consumption. This is merely to invent a new means of promoting conformity in our basic needs, a conformity which only declined in the age of liberalism. Traditionalist ages have always understood how to induce people through habits and customs to enjoy conformity in dress, food, and housing as more dignified than an aimless change. This unbridled craving for variety is not ingrained in human nature but is the product of the constant stimulation aroused by anarchic competition. In order to make additional profits one has to create new wants so that existing fashions soon become obsolete. . . . Freedom of thought in intellectual production is perfectly compatible with the standardisation of our primary needs (6).

This standardising of demand has occurred in many fields since the war, and according to Mannheim it had started before the war in cars, gas, wireless and electricity. Though it is possible that what he noted was only the creation of monopoly—and private monopolies lead to higher prices and a less efficient product.

Nor is wireless a good example of the standardising of demand; in 1938 there were 241 sets on a 'saturation' market made by twenty-four firms, a range offering a multiplicity that makes deliberate choice impossible and exemplifying rather the senseless and wasteful proliferation that must be avoided (7). Mannheim declares, of the trend to standardise demand, that 'this method of stimulating demand is exactly what a planned but unregimented society should aim at: inducing conformity not by authority or inculcation, but by skilful guidance, which allows the individual every opportunity for making his own decisions.'

II. Its use to society

There are some examples of responsible and socially useful advertising in the last few years, coming from commercial firms displaying a discerning self-interest, or from alert government departments. The working-class household, for instance, owing to such factors as lack of space and time, inadequate education and equipment, did not in peace time buy the best foods available for the money or make the best use of it when it got it. This clearly was of some concern to the Gas Light and Coke Company, and in 1936 and later (under its enlightened publicity manager, Mr. S. C. Leslie) it produced a 'Nutrition Film' and followed it up with a campaign of lecture-demonstrations under the general heading 'Better Meals for the Money' (8). The demonstrators explained to working-class audiences the significance of protective foods, the principle of a balanced diet, and the best way to choose, buy and cook the meals involved. (A campaign such as this might, of course, be arranged to coincide with a rise in the price of gas.) In the United States the Metropolitan Life Insurance has been advertising health for thirty years, simply because it pays. The health and longevity of members improved, premiums have gone on longer and death claims have been postponed. It is said that the life expectation of its policy-holders has increased by 12·6 years on an average, compared with an improvement of 8·3 years in the general population of the U.S.A., between 1911 and 1933, and with an improvement of 7·38 years in Great Britain during the same period. The Metropolitan distributes health bulletins to school teachers, shows one-reel films and buys space in newspapers and magazines (9).

In this country excessive spending on advertised foods, the distortion or frustation by advertising of scientific discoveries and medical pronouncements, and the misleading of the poor and those who care for invalids, all necessitate (according to the PEP *Report on British Health Services*) counter measures, such as the 'Use your Health Services' Campaign, and the British Medical Association's advertised plan for 'A General Medical Service for the Nation' and milk publicity. (That the latter was necessary there was no doubt, but I do not know if the milk distributing interests had any share in the scheme; it did not, incidentally, produce any increase in the total consumption of milk in the three years 1935–7 (10). Till 1939 the English consumption of milk was only one-third that of Finland, a poorer country, while the price was the highest in Europe.) Another example was the prominent part given in the National Health Campaign of 1937 to persuading prospective mothers to get antenatal advice, a course hitherto taken by only half of them. One of the best conceived and best executed campaigns was that initiated by the Ministry of Food in 1940. At appropriate seasons it explained what sort of diet was desirable, what could be purchased to fulfil these conditions, and the best methods of cooking the accessible foods. That the country's

health was good during the winter may have been a coinci-
dence, but it is very likely that the Ministry's commercially
executed propaganda had something to do with it.

Much of the socially useful advertising of the kinds just
described should be employed in the future, anyhow for a
transitional period. Much of it, too, would not be necessary
in a state with a different distributive system; the milk and
the food campaigns would not have been required if the
country had based its diet on other than tinned and advertised foods, or if the principles and means of health had been
taught in schools. It must be emphasised that in the case of
health propaganda especially advertising is rather a roundabout and expensive method of spreading knowledge and
prompting action, and one of uncertain efficacy. That it has
to be resorted to implies that the proper channels, education,
the daily and periodical Press, are choked up. The information transmitted is necessarily scrappy and unco-ordinated,
the separate drives for health or whatnot, diffuse and lacking
a unifying social purpose. One extension which has been
proposed is that the big insurance companies should take to
advertising on American lines. Their huge resources are an
object of desire to the advertising men, and it is not surprising that the suggestion came from Sir William Crawford,
head of W. S. Crawford, Ltd., advertising agents. The idea
has also been approved by a disinterested authority, Dr.
Harry Roberts (9). Though to judge by the present ethical
standards of one or two of these companies, there would
have to be a change of heart before anything socially useful
came out of them.

In any future that we can see, whether we like it or not,
Governments are likely to use advertising. I am not thinking
of straight political propaganda used to promote a policy
not yet adopted by the electorate, but of the announcements
issued by Government departments. So we shall next consider some examples of Government advertising in this

century, and then discuss its future principles and potentialities.

The first notable example occurred in 1913, when the Army was short of 7,000 men to fill depleted regiments, and on the advice of Sir Hedley le Bas a comparatively modest campaign, costing between £3,000 and £4,000, brought in the required men. In 1914 the intention had been to raise 35,000 men by a September campaign, but when war broke out there was need for millions. At first, with the well-known poster 'Your King and Country Need You', a 100,000 men were asked for, and eventually, according to Sir Hedley, millions were raised. The army thus recruited was given a brand name, 'Kitchener's Army', because, in the words of the director of the campaign, 'As a business man I know the value of a good name—the good-will, if I may use the word, of a brand name.' The most successful posters have been cited earlier (p. 74).

In the interval between the wars the use of publicity by Government departments increased, though to what extent we cannot easily tell. It is an opportunity for a piece of research in Hansard, Official Reports and the Press. In 1940, for example, the Home Office and Ministry of Home Security had a Public Relations Officer, Lt.-Col. E. T. Crutchley, C.B., C.M.G., C.B.E., at a salary of £1,700, an assistant P.R.O. at £1,200, two Press Officers at £800, and one at £700. The B.B.C. has a P.R.O., salary unstated—it is worth recording that there is less information available about the B.B.C. than about any other Government or Public Office; the space it takes up in *Whitaker* is less than that given to the Government Chemist. And so one could go on.

The Press departments and the expenditure on advertising have naturally increased during the war, and some statistics were given in the chapter on the Press. The Ministry of Food series was well conceived and well carried out, but in other cases the execution was poor or the objective suspect or vague. Some of it was negative, and perhaps superfluous as well; at the Press Conference opening of the anti-gossip campaign, for instance, 'pressmen asked the Director-General to give examples of the harm done by gossip. As he could not produce any, he was asked for examples from the last war, but the reply to this was that the War Office had never revealed any' (11). The worst example was the series run by the Ministry of Information in the winter of 1940; its cynical dishonesty was of the kind one associates with Goebbels. Under such headings as *The New Magna Carta; The Greatest Crusade; Democratic Imperialism,* the general statement was made that 'There has been nothing like it (the British Empire) in the world before; it is a Commonwealth, a family of free nations.' 'Men and women of every colour', we were told, 'are working out their own destiny' and 'in this war they are fighting shoulder to shoulder of their own free will'. Separate advertisements dealt with India ('the 380 millions of her people join with the rest of the British Commonwealth . . .') and Africa ('these 60 million peoples of different races . . . spoke with one voice . . . proud of an Empire which they know is the guarantee of their freedom and progress'), and other constituents. The trouble with these statements is that they are not true, and that therefore they will mislead opinion, about India, for example. The support of the Indian peoples (I am not thinking of the Princes, whose hatred of democracy and—in some cases—treatment of their human possessions makes their opposition to Hitler anomalous) is more and more needed. But we have not yet got it—India was declared a belligerent without being consulted—and we shall not get it if British public opinion is to be kept complacent by such astounding assertions. 'Southern Rhodesia', said one advertisement, 'controls her own affairs'; but in fact native Africans there have neither democratic rights nor direct representation, and one could quote admissions made in Parliament showing that Nazi cruelty is not confined to Nazi conquests. Many other facts could be cited to show the falsity of the Ministry's professions. One does not expect its advertisements to mention the Johannesburg floggings for failure to pay the poll tax: but to say that 'Africans . . . are equal with us before the law' is a bit of effrontery. Ill-considered propaganda as misleading as this may have a boomerang effect, though like Goebbels' work it may pay in the short run. The campaign was a failure: after three months of it there was, for instance, no significant improvement in the number of people who knew the difference between a Dominion and a Colony (12).

A good deal of Government propaganda seems to have been ineffective. That aiming at an immediate objective is more easily measured, and here there have been some failures. A typical one was the injunction by poster not to travel on August Bank Holiday, 1942 ; the public seemed to take no notice at all. The advice to eat National or wholemeal bread to save shipping space and improve health was equally ineffective. One conclusion is that it is absurd, at least in war time, to use persuasion for such aims as the introduction of better bread or the limitation of travel. Measures should be taken, and if necessary explained by advertisements; there is no question of infringing democratic rights if Parliament is working.

It seems a little odd that while a Government takes the lives it requires it should use advertising to obtain binoculars, as it did in 1940. 55,000 were needed and a campaign costing £10,000 produced 45,000 at the time these figures were given in the House of Commons (30 January 1941). And it seems a misdirection of energy to issue, in the advertising columns of the Press, tender appeals to the controllers of capital to buy Defence Bonds—an inefficient method to date, and one that should be replaced by compulsion. Millions are spent on advertising the National Savings campaign; how much of this is necessitated or nullified by the advertisements of big stores inviting us to listen to their dance bands or fortune-tellers, announcing 'We are holding no Sale, but end-of-season reductions . . .' and at every turn stimulating the expenditure which the Government discourages.

When we come to campaigns aiming at remoter (increase of production) or vaguer ends (morale) the uses of advertisement are again limited. General exhortations to go to it are useless; what are needed, for instance, are direct talks and factual propaganda within the factories. The early slogans (Your Courage, Your Cheerfulness, Your Resolution Will Bring Us Victory) met with general disapproval, and the reaction became one of annoyance and exasperation, according to the reports of Mass-Observation. Even in the middle of 1941 their reports showed that only 18% of the men and women consulted thought that Government advertising was 'Good', while 40% of the men consulted thought that it was 'Bad' or 'Very Bad'.

1939 seems to have been the first occasion when a British government tried to test the impact of its publicity, when Mass-Observation was requested by the Ministry of Information to make a survey about the red 'morale' posters. Then in the spring of 1940 an organisation called Wartime Social Survey was set up—under the auspices of the National Institute of Social and Economic Research, in order that it might be independent of the Ministry. The intention was that it should gauge and record the state of public opinion, a necessary step if the Ministry's work was to be effective; for neither Parliament nor Press can be considered to be adequately in touch with the public mind. In the following ten months it made reports for various Ministries on such subjects as sleeping conditions in heavily raided areas, habits and opinions relevant to the planning of community feeding, and other topics on which detailed information is needed in deciding policy. In 1941, according to a letter of Prof. A. V.

Hill in the *New Statesman and Nation* (6 September 1941), various changes were made in the Survey, impairing the objectivity and independence of the work.

It is now possible to deduce the functions of Government advertising. A programme of public administration has to be explained to the people whose affairs are being managed. It is not enough that Governments should provide health, child-welfare and educational services; they should also see that the public knows what facilities exist. It is not enough merely to register their existence by notices on police-stations or the speeches of Ministers—not enough at present, that is. At the risk of repetition it should be added that such uses of advertisement are transitional, and necessitated by the rather too large number of distractions and claims on the public's attention, and by definite gaps in our general education. As Dr. Robson wrote, in the article already quoted:

> Government departments must find ways of getting information to the citizens who need to know what a programme means, how they can take advantage of it, what is required of them, why they should support it. Consent to the political principles by the representatives of the people in Parliament must be reinforced by acquiescence or assent to the administrative process by the people themselves on a much more widespread scale.

Assent perhaps is rather too negative a word: ideally one would substitute 'active support and critical interest'. Government services should not be mere 'hand-outs' to a passive body of people with no opinions and no feelings—except political passions at election times; they work all the better for the co-operation and vigilance of the public. 'A wider knowledge of the innumerable ramifications of modern Government activity has more than the immediate effect; it certainly helps to make the citizen more conscious of his citizenship in a free community' (13). Such participation in government by the governed would, of course, act as some sort of check upon the misuses of the resources of publicity which are discussed in other chapters. But before leaving the subject, I would like to give one further example of Government advertising.

According to Sir Stephen Tallents the publicity of the Post Office is directed to the selling of its services, ensuring that they are correctly used (addressing of letters, posting early for Christmas) and securing the good-will of the public (to reduce expenditure in dealing with ill-founded complaints). With these aims goes 'internal publicity' to enable the individual worker in the Post Office to acquire an understanding and a general view of the whole organisation (14). Assuming that such publicity does not mean lower wages for its servants, or increased charges to the public, and that it is not used to induce a complacent attitude towards it, a desirable form of advertising is exemplified here. An overorganised industrial state depersonalises relations; nightbaking perhaps would not be tolerated if more people were in contact with those who make their bread. People regard the dustman or the postman as a working part of the machinery they pay for, without much considering the convenience or working conditions of these servants. So that if Post Office publicity increases the public's sense of responsibility towards those who serve it, a social function is performed.

III. Reforms and safeguards

This section will put forward some proposals for the reform of advertising from within, and discuss the possibilities of legislation and education.

If the more responsible advertising agents were influential in the professional organisations they could establish a code of practice, just as the medical and legal professions observe certain rules quite apart from legal obligations. Groups of advertisers selling useful and related products in certain fields could greatly increase the social utility of advertising and lower its costs by establishing a co-operative information service for consumers. Of this there is an excellent example in the Building Centre; unprejudiced advice and information are given to those who consult, even when this means recommending a non-advertised product in a range where the layman is likely to be acquainted only with what is widely advertised. One activity of such information services would be the issuing of classified lists of products, such as those issued by the National Book Council, an organisation supported by publishers and others. (A small bone to be picked with the N.B.C. is that some of its lists are compiled by interested parties—the one for advertising is selected by the Advertising Association and records no book that is seriously critical of its subject.) Other examples are the classified lists of films, theatres and other amusements that used to appear in *What's On*, a London weekly; lists of hotels and guest houses issued by travel bureaux, and the local classified directories of trades and businesses, issued by authority of the Post Office.

Another activity in which the advertising agencies might take part is a Census of Distribution, such as that carried out in the U.S.A. in 1930. In this country little is known of the relative importance of different channels of distribution, the number of shops and what they sell. That this lack is more than a nuisance to a few producers was evident in the maldistribution of produce in 1941; in travelling that year I found, not only that local shortages existed for a time—as everyone knows—but that such shortages persisted for months and were in fact permanent. A certain town would never have any saccharine, while in another it was plentiful and shopkeepers apologised if it was necessary to offer less than hundreds. In another town the bakers never had dried fruit for cakes, and there were always queues for such cakes

M

as there were, while supplies in a neighbouring county were excellent. Clearly the advertising agencies could have helped here, if they had had the information to offer. The cost of such a census (according to Mr. Hugh Weeks) would be up to £750,000, under 1% of the annual expenditure on all forms of advertising (15). As the same writer noted, such a census would be preliminary to a replanning of distribution aiming at a clear saving of £100,000,000 a year. Certain savings might be effected at once. In agriculture, for example, a 'distributive census would show the unrelated courses of the multiplicity of channels by which farm products now reach the consumer. The census would disclose some of the sources of waste and the magnitude of the interests involved.'

Another potentially useful task for the agencies is the market survey. I am aware, of course, that such surveys on a small scale and of varying ability have been carried out, but some of them at least have been of no value except to bluff some gullible client that in consulting |the agency he was getting something for his money. Market surveys have been needed and will be needed. It was desirable, for instance, that the milk consumption of this country should increase; but it seemed fantastic that large sums should have been spent to push its sales in a paper like the *Daily Telegraph*, the readers of which are mostly in an income range which consumes enough milk already. A genuine market survey would have avoided this waste, for which presumably the consumer pays in his milk bill. Such surveys may be valuable pieces of research, assembling useful information in one place for the first time; the writer, for example, learned from one of Messrs. Samson Clark's bulletins why electricity is so expensive in certain districts.

Another direction in which responsible producers and agencies could weed out deceitful advertising, possibly with the aid of legislation, is in the standardising of terminology, composition and quality. Some advertisers would oppose this because it would check the extension of branding and diminish the pulling power of many existent trade-marks. In some markets the brands don't deceive; we all know that one cigarette is as good as another at the same price and one beer as bad as another. In others we have found that simple substances or products (e.g. raisins), no better and possibly worse than others of the same kind, can be stuck in the public preference by the advertising of a brand and the pretension to some unique attribute. At present the consumer buys words instead of goods at a large part of the price per package. Pepper is just pepper, black or white—but salt at the average grocer's is a packed and branded substance, rendered impure by the addition of chemicals to make it run, lacking the sparkle, flavour and cheapness of block salt. From examples already current we can imagine extensions—'Don't buy salt, get SALLY'; 'Don't eat bread, buy BOAFERS—chunks of grainy honest-to-goodness nourishment. Kiddies love it— its nutty flavour saves butter. And watch the sparkle in their eyes! Scientific baking keeps the vitamins. . . . Buy a BOAFER now!' This process is almost a means of creating credulity and ignorance, and it will be difficult for those who use or live on advertising to refrain from exploiting a vein not as yet worked out.

The principle of buying goods on specification could be extended on lines exemplified by the British Standards Institution, an independent body supported by the Government but free from Government control. For the benefit of the building, engineering, chemical and textile trades it issues standard specifications which 'safeguard purchasers by ensuring a generally suitable quality and performance at a reasonable price . . . they help to eliminate redundant qualities and sizes and enable manufacturers to provide stock during slack periods and purchasers to obtain their requirements more rapidly' (16). This, of course, is a very summary account and omits the various safeguards against over-standardisation, unwise standards, etc. It costs about £36,000 p.a., to which the Government contributes £3,000, and industry by voluntary services indirectly contributes about £40,000 p.a. This seems a modest total compared with some of the figures already given for advertising. Most of its specifications are not of interest to the general reader, but a few of its results may be mentioned:

The international standard of concert pitch has been based on a frequency of 440 cycles per second for the note A in the treble clef.

British Standards for Controlled Cod Liver Oil Mixture.

A standard method for the biological assay of Vitamin D_3.

Specification for the Rating and Testing of Domestic Electrical Refrigerators.

A report on garment sizes for children and adults, with a view to standardising.

One of the most successful and least known achievements in standardising has been achieved by the Ormskirk Potato Research Station. Its primary work was to test all varieties of potato for susceptibility to wart disease, but in surveying existing varieties a surprising state of affairs was revealed. Hundreds of attractive names were being used to describe a few definite varieties of potato, and scores of so-called distinct varieties were actually identical. The National Institute of Agricultural Botany appointed a committee to investigate this, with Dr. R. N. Salaman as chairman. In *Nature* for 16 November 1940 he described what they discovered: 'The extent of the evil may be gauged by the fact that we found in existence some two hundred synonyms for the variety Up-to-date, and more than ninety each for Abundance and British Queen, whilst many seedsmen's catalogues recorded in glowing terms the superiority of the synonym to the mother stock, with which it had not infrequently shared the same sack in the storehouse. In general the synonym was priced at anything from 20 to 50% or more higher than the original.'

When the eyes of the trade were opened to the evils of synonymity, its magnitude and universality, an improvement was rapidly brought about. Not before time, because, as Dr. Salaman says, 'The monotony of normal trading might occasionally be broken by some financial boom, the most notorious of which occurred a few years before the Ormskirk activities began. On this occasion an inferior stock of an inferior variety was renamed Eldorado and sold for its weight in gold to a public only too ready to be beguiled. The excitement, the credulity, the folly and the fraud, together with the final dénouement, resembled the South Sea Bubble in miniature.'

There have, of course, been some efforts to standardise quality. The Full Fruit Standard, suspended in war time, was even in peace time much too low; 30–40% was the amount fixed by arrangement between the Food Manufacturers' Association and the Society of Public Analysts. A form of deception which should be eliminated, according to the National Federation of Grocers' and Provision Dealers' Associations, is the 'odd-weight pack' for jam, marmalade and jelly; we are most of us familiar with the 'No. 2 jar' of some manufacturers which looks as if it contains two pounds (17). Schemes such as the National Mark Grading Scheme and the Seeds Act might be applied to other goods. The label 'Tested in accordance with the provisions of the Seeds Act, 1920. Germination and purity are not less than the minimum percentages prescribed by the Seeds Regulations, 1921' cannot be used to dispose of bad stuff.

We come now to the possibilities of legislating against the excesses of advertising. At the moment there are few laws directly affecting advertising. The Indecent Advertisements Act of 1889 is directed against obscene advertisements, specifically against those relating to venereal disease; it is probably a dead letter now. The Advertisements Regulation Act of 1907 gives any local authority the power to make by-laws for the control of hoardings higher than twelve feet, and to prohibit advertisements which destroy natural beauty. These powers were extended and clarified by the Advertisements Regulation Act of 1925, to include the protection of views of rural scenery, the amenities of villages, historic buildings and places frequented for their beauty or historic interest, though the amenities of a well-planned town were not apparently considered at all. This Act has produced excellent results in the country. In the U.S.A. many states have statutes against hoardings, and in Pennsylvania 30,000 were removed in a fortnight; in some of the eastern states a threatened boycott by women caused the removal of most hoardings near railway lines. In New Zealand certain towns have by-laws absolutely forbidding posters.

In financial advertising, the prospectus announced in the Press must follow exactly the official prospectus deposited at Somerset House, both in wording and layout. If the prospectus is not illustrated, the advertisement must not be illustrated. The law says that there shall be no misrepresentation in the prospectus, and as the latter is always scrutinised by lawyers for any loophole, there is no scope for enthusiastic copywriting. There is further precedent for the restriction of undesirable advertising in the Moneylenders Act of 1926, which prohibits moneylenders from advertising any inducement to do business with them; their announcements are limited by law to a statement of their name, address and nature of the business carried on.

More bills to restrict advertising have been drafted than have reached the statute book. Many local by-laws against posters have been defeated or diluted by the well-organised opposition of the bill-posting interests. The Advertisements Regulation Bill of 1919 and another of the same title in 1921, giving Local Authorities power to remove all hoardings, failed—'the fight was short and so far as the trade is concerned, immediately successful.' (Sheldon, *History of Poster*

Advertising.) The interests which profit from advertising appear to be particularly well defended in Parliament, to judge from the history of the Pharmacy and Medicines Bill. Though in its various forms it prohibited the advertising of cures for serious or incurable diseases, such as cancer or tuberculosis, it has failed to become law on four occasions since 1920. The Food and Drugs Bill prepared by the Local Government and Public Health Consolidation Committee in 1937 contains some checks upon the fraudulent advertisement of proprietary remedies. It penalises the selling of 'any food or drug which is not of the nature or not of the substance, or not of the quality' of the product demanded, but excludes proprietary medicines supplied in response to a demand. It also makes it an offence to publish an advertisement 'which falsely describes any food or drug, or is otherwise calculated to mislead as to its nature, substance or quality.'

The principles of these measures and of the law about financial advertising should be extended to many products other than food or drugs, to ensure so far as possible that no fraudulent claims are made in advertisements, and that goods are described with reasonable accuracy. It should be possible to devise workable measures, though the quality of all goods cannot be ascertained as accurately as in the case of seeds or simple homogeneous substances. Further action could be taken on the lines of those by-laws which limit the size and colour of advertisements. In the Derbyshire Peak for instance the use of petrol signs is restricted, and the name of a garage occupier or owner may only be displayed once and then in letters nor more than 12 ins. high. In many rural districts all petrol pumps have to be a uniform green. Now that hoardings are being removed in war time for their timber, and paper is short, let us see that they do not re-appear; we shall need after the war to cut down imports of timber and pulp, and here is an opportunity, quite apart from the need for freedom from posters in the new post-war towns we are promising ourselves. Illuminated signs and hoardings sited at skew bridges to attract the motorist's eye should both be banned; there is no doubt that they have caused many accidents. If we accept the principle that the mere physical assault of advertising on our senses should be limited—robbery with violence is worse than plain robbery, and it usually wouldn't succeed without the violence—there is every reason for the restriction of posters to double-crown size, and possibly for fixing a relation between the maximum size of displayed advertisements and the size of the newspaper page that exhibits them. Newspapers, too, might be required to take some further responsibility for the contents of their advertising space. From a glance at war-time papers it looks as if advertisers were competing for space, rather than being solicited to buy; if this inversion of peace conditions continues, the Press will go a long way towards recovering its independence.

The possibility of taxing advertisements should also be mentioned. Till 1853 newspapers used to pay a tax of 1s. 6d. on each advertisement published, and the revival of this and the imposition of additional taxation has been urged by some critics. For instance, the PEP *Report on the Press* considers possible a graduated tax on Press advertising designed to fall most heavily upon large circulation newspapers. During the 1914–18 war a tax on posters, for revenue-raising purposes, was proposed, and the Press concealed all mention of the suggestion lest newspaper advertising should also be tapped. However, 'the industry took action' (Sheldon, op. cit.) and no more was heard of the proposal. More recently Mr. Clough Williams-Ellis has advocated a tax upon hoardings graded in inverse ratio to the rateable value of the land or building. He believes that manufacturers generally would welcome an enforced advertising holiday, but that the advertising interests are so powerful that the actual producers are unlikely to gain their freedom for many years. In the U.S.A. fourteen states impose taxes on hoardings; here they are subject only to income tax normally assessed under Schedule A on annual value.

The uses of legislation are limited, and mainly negative. But it has distinct uses in the transitional period. It looks as if advertising as a social incubus has much diminished in the present war, but we may find that after it there will be recrudescence of the worse forms. That is why gradual, piecemeal legislation may be a profitable oblique approach to the problem, and a means of focussing and educating public attention. By-laws preserving the country were one such step, Mr. A. P. Herbert's 1938 Bill against sky-writing would have been another, and the Pharmacy and Medicines Bill of 1941 represents a decided advance. A further important step would be more adequate protection for the consumer against products which fail to fulfil their claims. On the other hand, it has been pointed out to me that it is otiose to suggest the reforms proposed here, on the ground that they are impossible under the present industrial system.

Where consumers have not the technical knowledge or apparatus to test the conflicting claims of foods, or where it is hardly the Government's business to nurse the consumer, as in the car market, something of the nature of a Consumers' Union is needed. This American organisation is supported by thousands of consumers (55,000 at one time, but I have not any recent figures) and has its own staff, laboratories and consultants. General and Confidential Bulletins have been issued, each number usually devoted to a particular field— food, clothing, toilet goods—of competing products. The information has been valuable even to an English subscriber, because apart from the presence in both countries of similar methods and products the work is not merely critical; where an advertised product is expensive or bad, alternative methods and substances are recommended, and detailed formulas and instructions given. There is no reason why a similar service should not be started here, though the present working of the libel laws would require it to be circumspect. As Professor J. B. S. Haldane said several years ago:

> Enormous sums are spent in advertising medicines and 'health foods' which are generally useless and often dangerous. A widely advertised vitamin preparation contains, besides vitamins, a substance definitely poisonous to children. Under the law of the land I might have to pay thousands of pounds in damages if I mentioned the preparation in question, even if my statement were true. On the other hand I am at liberty to say publicly that diphtheria anti-toxin is useless, which is a plain lie.

Reform in the libel law is badly needed. The raisin trade, for the sake of its profits, may advise you for years on end to eat raisins as a source of food iron, but a passing reference to some limitation of a commercial product—a point of trivial importance compared with the other—may bring down on the writer a battery of the most expensive and imposing lawyers.

We train our children in road-sense, and we should with equal application bring them up in such a way that they will not be run over by juggernaut advertising. It would be progress indeed if schools provided an education enabling pupils, as a minimum, to discriminate between informative and persuasive advertising. This should be a normal development of teaching how to read; in elementary schools at present the instruction in reading stops just at the point where further direction is required. It is commonplace that children who leave school at fourteen to start earning pathetically and prematurely acquire adult habits. Further training should be imparted not only as a protection against exploitation by commercial interests, but also as inoculation against propaganda, because, as Bertrand Russell observed, 'the whole modern technique of government in all its worst aspects is derived from advertising'. Understanding of the methods and function of advertising is not an end in itself; it positively helps a child's development, and must form part of any education which brings its pupils into vital relation with their environment.

Mr. Russell in a pamphlet *Education for Democracy* (publ. Association for Education in Citizenship) has made some proposals for combating the technique of producing irrational belief, as perfected by advertisers:

> I should start very young. If I had to run an infant school, I should have two sorts of sweets—one very, very nice and the other very, very nasty. The very nasty ones should be advertised with all the skill of the most able advertisers in the world. On the other hand, the nice ones should have a coldly scientific statement, setting forth their ingredients and consequent excellence. I should let the children choose which they would have. I should of course vary the assortment from day to day, but after a week or two they would probably choose the ones with the coldly scientific statement. That would be one up. I should go on in the same way all through.

Mr. Aldous Huxley has made very similar suggestions in his *Ends and Means*. The present writer has practised training in the analysis of advertisement and oratory with his pupils for several years, on lines indicated in *Culture and Environment* (1932) and *Between the Lines*. This has been done, not as a stunt, but as a normal part of teaching English; and I believe from the records of experiments in *English in Schools* (18) that others have gone much further and produced a technique, the use of which is spreading. The B.B.C., for example, gave a school broadcast on Advertising in 1941 with success, if this report from a senior school is typical:

> We were inclined to suspect its suitability to non-literary girls . . . we felt that no good could come from the talk. But we were quite wrong. From the first critical awareness of advertisement given by means of this broadcast we have had a sequence

of valuable work in English. At School dinner-tables ideas on advertisements have been put forward by girls whose normal small-talk is of the 'what lessons do you have this afternoon' quality. Collections of advertisements from local papers, old copies of *Punch*, etc., have been made, discussed, and classified as having 'fear' or 'snob' appeal. A girl who is not literary wrote freely and well in discussing why a pictured butler or the phrase '20 only' help to sell things. . . .

School Broadcasts—How We Use Them

It is not only in the work on the time-table that schools can deflate advertising; there are ways other than the academic or intellectual. In a school where the children are contented, where normal moral and spiritual growth is fostered and the influence of the school continues out of teaching hours, pupils should have an independence and health to make them proof against at least some of the advertiser's assaults. The ideal school will impart an outlook, a balanced attitude, a scheme of values wherein the advertisers' 'good time' will seem shoddy and unattractive. But it is evident that such an ideal school does not and cannot exist, yet. To a large extent the character of a school is determined by the society in which it exists; and though education is at least a point where something can be done to break the vicious circle, its potentialities are limited. Advertising, much of it, thrives on social maladjustments, and until they are corrected, some of the worst evils will remain. All advertising might be stopped to-day, but the emotional drives, prompted by advertising and readily working in a society where anxieties and frustrations occupy too much of life, would continue. Fear of old age, of unemployment, of what the neighbours are thinking of our curtains or our car, would still be with us. (The extension of Insurance and Health benefits to incomes up to £420 should remove some of the anxieties and fears.)

Whether, with our mass cities and mass life, we can recover a simpler, more resourceful, more independent mode of living needs to be discussed. The war, too, may have achieved something in partially removing tinned stuff, compelling us to use healthier foods and better cooking. The return to a peasant's diet suggests that there are other peasant virtues to be cultivated—avoiding the peasant vices of meanness, suspiciousness, narrowness and conservatism. Some of the reasons why advertising is only found on a small scale in France are the survival of a peasant outlook, scepticism about the written word, the skill of French cooks and their hostility to tinned and advertised products. Again, there are no salesmen in China, not only because of China's material poverty—a go-getter can get blood out of a stone—but also because the Chinese are a nation of peasants, taught by Confucius to be suspicious of eloquence of any sort, especially eloquence designed to part them from their money. In fact, as Carl Crow noted, 'the Master held up for special condemnation the very type of person who would qualify to-day as an ideal salesman, that is, a handsome, well-dressed man with a pleasing address. . . . It is impossible to conceive of a convention of Chinese salesmen, for everyone would be ashamed to attend it.' Generally, the peasant has to acquire a number of skills; his work and social life give him certain positive if limited satisfactions; traditions impart a degree of practicable wisdom, certain unformulated ideas about the ends of life, standards of conduct. At the other extreme we find in North America, where advertising has achieved its most startling successes, a people without roots, without standards other than those of an acquisitive society, without traditions except in an unrecognisably diluted solution. Into the breaches left unfilled by home or church or school the advertiser poured his suggestions.

CHAPTER VI

CAUTIOUS CONCLUSIONS

English civilisation is predominantly—of course not exclusively—based on the most powerful factors of the mass-mind, the will, and the egoistic and materialistic instincts. Its political institutions are democratic. This is possible because in England the population is less diversified in character than in most other countries. The constitution . . . depends on the assumption, peculiar to the Anglo-Saxon, that an entire nation will react, uniformly, to certain great mass-slogans, represented by a great man whom it trusts and reveres, and can be ruled through the machinery of suggestion represented in the Press. Advertisement technique—an Anglo-Saxon invention—corresponds in the economic sphere to this political slogan technique.

WILLIAM DIBELIUS, England, p. 498

ADVERTISING is a powerful engine for influencing masses of people by irrational appeals. As such it needs handling with care, and more research needs to be carried out on its potentialities. It is a concern of every individual, not only as a 'consumer', but as a citizen whose life is affected by the government he helps to choose from political parties. The latter, since 1930, have borrowed extensively from commercial advertising for their propaganda. For that reason we must discuss further non-commercial advertising—or propaganda—and some of the non-commercial effects of ordinary advertising. The imitation by propagandists of advertising method may have its dangers; is it safe or desirable to promote a policy on the same lines as you would push the sale of a patent medicine? It will be remembered that in the last war advertisers turned propagandists carried on a hate-campaign against the Germans, designed to maintain morale at home and keep up the fighting temper of the men at the front. It disgusted a good many soldiers, and in the very short run it worked at home. But public opinion at home was so inflamed with hatred and the desire for revenge that it proved impossible to make a rational reparations settlement.

We may expect to see advertising and its techniques more widely used by those who can command the necessary resources. We have seen the trend in the employment of public relations counsels, and the buying of advertising space, not for direct sales, but so that firms or organisations or individuals may secure public approval. In the last ten or fifteen years American publicity agents acting on behalf of the utilities especially have prepared thousands of 'ghost-written' interviews and magazine articles setting forth virtuous principles over their clients' signatures; supplied editors with thousands of camouflaged advertisements in the form of news-stories; and subsidised lecturers, professors and writers of text-books (19). Mr. F. L. Allen, in *Lords of Creation*, gives an example: 'One organisation in Oregon prepared "canned" editorials on the iniquity of public ownership of utilities and similar topics, distributed them to local newspapers all over the country, got thousands of them published, ostensibly as spontaneous expressions of editorial opinion—and for this service was paid $84,000 in four years by interested companies.' Again in 1936 the pressure exerted by big business against Roosevelt at the presidential elections was so clumsy that, according to American observers, it had a considerable boomerang effect. But by 1940 the anti-Roosevelt campaign was being conducted by professional publicity men.

In this country, evidence is hard to come by; only the more overt attempts can be cited. At the time of the Spanish Civil War, the owners of ships trading to Spain bought space to protest against that particular form of non-intervention which allowed the Italians to bomb and sink British merchantmen. In 1938 the railways expended hundreds of thousands of pounds on advertising their need for a square deal, and this was followed in 1939 by legislation strengthening the railways' position in relation to road transport and in other years by pleasing results for shareholders. In 1938, too, the owners' Mining Association of Great Britain covered a good acreage of paper with protests against Part Two of the Coal Bill, which dealt with compulsory amalgamation. The employment of an advertising agency to build up Mr. Chamberlain's reputation we have already mentioned; and it will be remembered that in January 1940 the *Daily Express* and the *Evening Standard* published advertisements demanding the recall of Mr. Hore-Belisha to the War Office. Other papers refused these advertisements, which were said to have been paid for by a well-known public figure.

This new development is of some interest; it shows that the only way, apart from broadcasting, of quickly reaching the huge masses that make up 'public opinion' is now the Press. Whether it is a reliable one is uncertain, but there are two objections to it: one, that the newspapers exert their own censorship; two, that even this somewhat muzzled form of free speech is so costly that it is free only to those with thousands of pounds to spare; this means that the minority groups, which often hold views that the nation will hold tomorrow, are debarred from reaching any but a converted public. Another possibility is that such mass-appeals may only succeed if they use slogans and emotionalism, directed to the L C M of public opinion; if this is so, we shall tend to have a society of individuals incapable of thought and conditioned to a purely collective response. The expense of such publicity makes it easy for a concern or an individual to gain a high degree of immunity from criticism; it is one-sided, and there is no possibility of a public reply. The same objections apply to government advertising; it may be used to conceal inefficiency or bureaucratic domination or to retain power for a government which no longer deserves support. And as Dr. Robson[1] noted, 'great watchfulness is needed, especially in war time, to see that legitimate administrative publicity does not gradually develop into full-blown control over the discussion of political and military affairs.' None of our present political parties could be trusted with a monopoly of advertising resources, and we shall need to watch carefully the possibility that the Ministry of Information may be used to gain or keep power for a government afraid to be judged on its merits.

One remedy against the semi-dictatorship that might be assisted by the pressure-group advertising just described would be a Press more nearly independent of advertising revenue. Complete independence may be a counsel of perfection, though it would be possible to run a daily completely free from advertising, like the American *P.M.* A writer in the *Economist* (16 January 1937) has calculated that if advertisements were abolished in a paper of twelve editorial and eight advertising pages, it would have either to increase its circulation to 5,000,000 or reduce its editorial pages to six. The war has accustomed us to smaller newspapers, and some readers may hope that we shall never return to the more and more comprehensive magazines and guides to life in general that advertising made possible; we can surely do without the astrology, the potted philosophy and the gossip column. There is everything to be said for getting the Press out of the big business field, and leaving it to be run by men with more responsibility and dignity than the ex-cement kings and others who have invaded Fleet Street. There are plenty of actual and potential editors and plenty of journalists who are sick and cynical at the work they have to do. If the Press could secure comparative independence of advertising, the public mind would be in a much healthier state, with all kinds of salutary effects. It was freedom of criticism that changed a Chamberlain into a Churchill government, just in time. But an emancipated Press would earlier have registered the necessary change of feeling and opinion. A free Press, too, might accept advertisements, commercial or political, and criticise them in its editorial columns. This freedom too might obviate another contingency. During the war the government in the national interest has assumed the control of certain private profit-making concerns, and it seems likely that post-war reconstruction will necessitate the development of this state capitalism. After 1918 there was a rowdy Press campaign for the benefit of advertisers to secure an immediate return to private ownership, and many useful controls and schemes were prematurely and wastefully broken up. The question now arises: are the comparable problems of this new post-war period to be settled on their merits or at the behest of an interested minority? We may find, for instance, that a post-war government decides that the experience gained during the war will point to the need for a continued decentralisation of industry, for large public housing schemes, for the continuance, temporary or permanent, of government control of food distribution and of publicly owned restaurants. It is quite easy to envisage a Press campaign, conducted at the instigation of advertisers, calling for the immediate end of all state and social controls. Readers of the *Daily Mail* in 1919 will be able to coin a few slogans. To take the profit-motive out of the supply of news and views would save us from the caprice of the *Napoleons manqués* who have cornered Fleet Street.

We may some time get a government or a party determined to keep on after the war the social services brought in as emergency measures, and resolved to end a state of affairs wherein resources are only used if the process is profitable to financial interests. If so, we may expect a good deal of advertising to educate the public mind in the new principles and their practice. It will be interesting to see if this can happen. Up to the present there is no instance of a radical change of opinion moulded in the channels of advertising, perhaps because the technique has not been seriously applied. Advertising commonly follows changes in public opinion or feeling; it capitalises some event or pronouncement or shift in popular attitudes, and in this way it may formulate opinions in its readers.

So far advertising has not directed public opinion on particular issues, but it has affected attitudes towards the social structure, and our behaviour and habits of thinking. We may be influenced even by advertising intended perhaps to capture good-will, which is pleasant in itself. For example, no-one could be anything but grateful for the many series of excellent posters with which the L.P.T.B. used to decorate the entrances to its stations; presumably they were part of the policy which made the Underground famous for functional designing. It might be said too that the Press advertisements of the Transport Board, recording number of miles run and passengers carried, were a desirable piece of public relations work. On the other hand it could be argued that if the aim were to conceal facts about profits, wages and working conditions and to keep in the background such problems as the uncontrolled swelling of London, it could hardly be more effectively achieved. Silence, the means of controlling the public's mental agenda, is a most potent form of propaganda.

Advertising is naturally in favour of the *status quo;* and advertisements are often aimed at the middle class. Here is an advertisement which appeared in the twenty years' armistice:

> Those who remember pre-war days have probably noticed how the England we knew is returning once again. The old friendly smile is reappearing on the faces of passers-by. The newspaper-seller calls us 'sir' without effort. The shopkeeper takes our small order with cheerful courtesy.
>
> This change in spirit has come, I believe, to stay . . . England

in those pre-war days was a fine place to work and play in. There was income to be earned, true sociability, unforced laughter. Few save the rich ventured far on the creaking stairway of social ambition: only the inexperienced strove for that class equality that will finally come on Judgment Day. We were permitted to appreciate books and wine and music without being ballyhooed as intellectuals.

Advert in Food Technology

—and part of another which appeared in The Times in 1937:

TO-DAY'S CONDITIONS
AND THE
PROPERTY OWNER

These are difficult days—days for cool heads and clear thinking, days for resolute courage and keen foresight, days for industriousness and a calm confidence in those who guard the interests of the Nation. For it is well to acknowledge that troublesome times have been encountered in the past, and that it has been in those very periods of uncertainty the National morale has asserted itself . . .

From the point of view of the British manufacturer, one of the most perplexing problems during recent months has been the reticence of the public to buy certain classes of commodities —although the wherewithal to do so has not been lacking. Yet the position in so far as Paint products are concerned is indicative of a commendable soundness of outlook on the part of the Property Owner.

Both these are class appeals, consolidating class feeling. Other advertisements less directly but firmly supporting the *status quo* are aimed at a wider public. Here are some extracts from beer advertisements, not confined to middle-class papers:

(Illustration displaying two glasses and two darts)

Around these glasses all subjects are discussed but no angry fists are thumped. No foreign beards are wagged, or dangerous doctrines spread. . . . No heads are cracked, but only jokes. For this is the drink of a free people—ale or stout, the drink of our Nation and of sport and peaceful life.

It may be recalled here that in 1938 the bill-posting firms refused to handle anti-Chamberlain propaganda. Somewhat similar efforts to preserve things as they profitably were then, were made in the U.S.A. when the advertising bosses campaigned against Roosevelt's third term—without having to be hired. The amendments to the Food and Drug Laws and the activities of the Federal Trade Commission in correcting the flaws of advertising have embittered them ever since the President's first years. Proprietary remedies and foods were among their wealthiest clients and the effort to protect the public from misleading advertising seemed to them an assault on the capitalist order. Advertisers, too, consistently discriminated against publications supporting Mr. Roosevelt.

After the war there may be a demand for a return to the 1939 standard of living. Already at the time of writing (1942) advertisements are appearing which are stimulating and cashing in on the expectations of the new world as envisaged by the makers of cars and soap. One starts with picture of girl leaning over the photographic studio's length of deck railing: 'The great liners cross the painted oceans. . . . On board are games and merry laughter and tinkling drinks with ice and *lemons!* . . . this is *the new world*. . . . Transport has its part to play in the new world—on sea, in the air, on land. There will be fine new roads in the land and fine new cars on them.' The soap-maker is equally lyrical:

> When we think of the evil forces which are challenging our race, we can reflect with pride on the united effort we are making for victory. Then out of this spurred effort will also come a great impetus to scientific progress after the war—an impetus which will give to a Britain at peace better health, better homes, a better standard of living and a happier life for all.

One is led to speculate whether these visionary copy-writers are merely ignorant of, or actually trying to counter the feelings which really are possessing the masses at whom the announcements are directed. In any case they are anti-social, distracting attention from reality. They keep going the feeling that things are going on much as usual in spite of the war; in Germany, on the other hand, retailers are required to use window displays for educative graphs, and not to create desires or evoke memories of peace (*Planning*, No. 188). According to a Mass-Observation bulletin of the same period 'There is a considerable depression about post-war prospects among many trades and jobs. The pattern of industrial worry is related to the post-war job worry. People are still visualising an end to this war modelled on 1918 and the following years, with unfulfilled promises, trade slumps and unemployment. They are expecting a post-war world where the process of job-getting and attaining economic security are similar to those in 1939.'

Suppose that a return to the 1939 standard will not be immediately possible after the war, even for those who have the money to spend, or that the post-war government finds it necessary to maintain for a time or make more general the lower but adequate standard that many put up with during the war. Or suppose that this lower standard may be dictated by the conditions of international trade or the need for physical reconstruction at home. Or suppose merely that the government insists on more equitable distribution of goods. The question in any case is, 'Will the frame of mind induced by advertising support these hypothetical conditions?' It is at least tenable that one of the less consciously produced effects of advertising is the way in which the development of a healthy public opinion is thwarted by the insistence of advertisements on the importance of self, especially as expressed in the possession of things. The individual is reminded again and again of his rights; or of such rights as may be exercised with profit to a vendor, but never of his responsibilities. In this way civic sense, social conscience, and genuine patriotism are crowded out; there is no room left for a sense of responsibility or altruism. Advertising is not being detached as a scapegoat; political parties make the same mistake in having no conception other than that of economic man, swayed mainly by his own self-interest and acquisitiveness.

When we consider the means of reorganising society, we find that, because thought and energy are dissipated elsewhere, apathy is the normal attitude towards politics, except at general elections. At these the habits of mind shown in buying goods are transferred to the business of choosing a representative. Members of Parliament are often elected for reasons as relevant as those which determine the selection of soap or cigarettes. I always remember one successful candidate whose chief positive appeal was a pretty wife and child, charmingly photographed on his election address; his other plank was a warning against 'The all-Red Route to Ruin'. Political discussion is carried on at the advertising level. It had descended to this in Germany, where, as E. A. Mowrer noted (20) about the rise of the Nazis: 'By isolation, repetition and complete disregard for objective truth, it proved as easy to sell political theories to the less developed as to sell pink pellets or blue razor blades.' More will be said of the relation between politics and advertising, but for the moment it need only be added that both commercial and non-commercial advertising are often in the same hands. For instance, shortly before the war the propaganda campaigns for Guinness, Gold Flake and the National Government Publicity Bureau, to say nothing of Johnny Walker, the Treasury, Austin Cars and the War Office, were all in the hands of one agency.

Before we examine the resemblances between advertising and political propaganda, it ought to be said that a qualified judge, Prof. F. C. Bartlett, in his *Political Propaganda*, considers that in the last twenty or thirty years advertisements have become more intellectually interesting. What makes a man think for himself, he says, is having a lot of different courses of action thrust upon him at once, or in rapid succession each presented as the best; 'sooner or later the ordinary person is pretty well bound to try to look fairly at the different possible lines of action and then decide fairly for himself.' This seems an over-optimistic view of human capabilities, and one for which some evidence is required.

I would like now to illustrate the parallel between advertising and political propaganda by examples from Nazi Germany. As early as 1932, when he was trying to impress the world and scare the Germans into submission, Goebbels declared that in his campaign for Hitler in the presidential elections he would use 'American methods on an American scale'. (When he lost he protested that the other side had won by brazen employment of commercial methods.)

First, as to the principles: both advertising and propaganda must be addressed to the masses:

> When advertising, think of the masses. Practise Mass Psychology.
>
> ELWYN O. HUGHES, *An Outline of Advertising*

> Propaganda must always address itself to the broad masses of the people ... its purpose must be exactly that of the advertisement poster, to attract the attention of the masses.
>
> HITLER, *Mein Kampf*, Hurst and Blackett edition of 1939

In both cases the appeals must be made at a low intellectual level:

> Copy should tax no-one's intelligence. The audience is too vast. You don't select your audience from the few; you appeal to the many.
>
> GILBERT RUSSELL, *Advertisement Writing*

All propaganda must be presented in a popular form and fix its intellectual level so as not to be above the heads of the least intellectual of those to whom it is directed. Thus its purely intellectual level will have to be that of the lowest mental common denominator among the public it is desired to reach. When there is a question of bringing a whole nation within the reach of its influence . . . too much attention cannot be paid to the necessity of avoiding a high level.

Mein Kampf

But it's best to appeal to the instincts and emotions:

Appeal to reason in your advertising and you appeal to about 4 per cent. of the human race. Appeal to instinct and you can touch everyone, from the Australian aborigine to the most highly developed product of twentieth-century civilisation.

Advertising and Selling

'Emotional' copy is now very widely used. It forms an appeal to the reader's emotions: fear, sympathy, pride, animosity or to whatever fundamental instinct it may react upon.

ELWYN O. HUGHES, *An Outline of Advertising*

[The aim of propaganda is not] to dispense individual instructions to those who already have an educated opinion on grounds of objective study—because that is not the purpose of propaganda, it must appeal to the feelings of the public rather than to their reasoning powers.

Mein Kampf

Reiteration is a main weapon:

Poor values can be sold by large persistent advertising. It is simply a question of psychology—the hammering into people's minds of a certain idea until finally they accept it.

E. A. FILENE, quoted in Taylor, *Economics of Advertising*

Slogans should be persistently repeated until the very last individual has come to grasp the idea that has been put forward.

Mein Kampf

Slogans should be employed because:

> A headline which contains not more than five words is most likely to be taken in by the hurried reader.
>
> HAROLD HERD, *Bigger Results from Advertising*

> The receptive powers of the masses are very restricted, and their understanding is feeble. On the other hand they quickly forget. Such being the case, all effective propaganda must be confined to a few details and those must be expressed as far as possible in stereotyped formulas.
>
> *Mein Kampf*

Another cardinal point:

> 'Behind every man there is a woman.' Don't underestimate this in your advertising. Have your advertisements up and examine them from this point of view. We in Crawfords are ceaselessly studying 'the appeal to women'. For only with such knowledge, and by making the fullest use of it, do we find that advertising may be made to pull the biggest possible sales.
>
> ADVERTISEMENT FOR W. S. CRAWFORD

> The great majority of a nation is so feminine in its character and outlook that its thought and conduct are ruled by sentiment rather than by sober reasoning. This sentiment, however, is not complex, but simple and consistent. It is not highly differentiated, but has only the negative and positive emotions of love and hatred, right and wrong, truth and falsehood. Its notions are never partly this and partly that. English propagandists especially understood this in a marvellous way and put what they understood into practice.
>
> *Mein Kampf*

There are many tactical affinities, too. From the happy ending stories in the adverts of how the Typist married the Boss, how Jim found Fun and Friends by ingesting a fruit salt, how some Built Muscle and others got £10 a Week for Life by taking Mind-training courses, we know that a principal approach of advertising is to dangle Success in front of the public's face. This accords with the principle enunciated by Elwyn O. Hughes in his *Outline of Advertising*: 'Desire. Conjure up in the reader's mind a wish, desire, even a craving for your merchandise. Show him how it will ease his work and make his life more tolerable, give him increased interest, the joy of possession, and, holding him in the grip of desire, compel him to act.' Many observers have noted that in Germany too the people were led by the nose when the Nazis offered Success. Stephen Roberts found that: 'Goebbels from his radio-base in Munich continues to make use of the siren-call of German economic prosperity ("Join us and double your wages!") and to titillate the feeling of German superiority by pointing to new German successes in the diplomatic field' (21).

Stephen Roberts also describes how Goebbels' propaganda, seemingly fully documented by word and picture, triumphs over reason. 'Every investigator in Germany feels this—whatever his beliefs may be, the constant repetition of propaganda, in the Press, on the air, and through personal media, wears down his resistance, until he has to exert a conscious effort not to acquiesce in a campaign he would instantly question if considering it aloofly in his own study in his own country.' And there is no need to quote much to show that advertising works in the same way, and the advertising men know it—cf. quotation from *Nuntius*: *Advertising and its Future* on p. 93. Just as Goebbels is said to have arrived at a mathematical relationship between the stream of propaganda and any individual's power of resistance, and (in his early days at least) had the public's reaction to every poster tested and the posters removed overnight if unsuitable, so the advertisers try to be 'scientific':

Advertising is becoming increasingly exact every day. Where instinct used to be enough, it is being replaced by inquiry. Advertising men nowadays don't say, 'The public will buy this article from such and such a motive': they employ what is called market research to find out the buying motives, as exactly as time and opportunity permit, from the public itself.

The close parallel between principles and practice of advertising here and propaganda there is instructive. I do not know what are the latest figures for the German expenditure on propaganda, but it is doubtful if they exceed the normal aggregate for British expenditure on advertising in peace time. The British effort is directed at moulding the buying behaviour of the public, and perhaps at securing public acquiescence in a state of affairs profitable to advertisers: the German at influencing political behaviour and ensuring support for the régime. If the volumes of persuasion to which the nations are subjected are comparable, are the results, too, likely to be entirely disparate? The German masses, we are told, have ceased to think; but we should be rash if we assumed a great margin of superiority here. Educated persons, especially those who wish to spread political or religious beliefs, have often too high an opinion of the reasoning power, and a misconception of the interests of the masses they seek to convert. Anyone inclined to reject this assertion out of hand should study some of the material collected by Mass-Observation at elections or crises. They reveal ignorance, credulity, apathy, on an astounding scale.

Advertising goes on all the time: political activity is spasmodic. It is at least possible that the persistent activity of the one determines the currency of the other, so that in politics the familiar methods of advertising are staple, and rational second thought is excluded. Often the appeal of both is to the imitative, credulous, timid sub-conscious self, which lacks individuality and self-control. (The relationship between advertising and the currency of politics need not be explained as cause and effect; both are symptoms of the same *malaise*.) If people are conditioned to mainly gregarious reactions, and habituated to emotional beliefs and over-simplified thinking, they cease to think or exist as individuals. Over-development of the gregarious habit in man will prevent 'progress', because it will fail to use the energy and intelligence of individuals. Instead of thinking for ourselves, we shall—as we did with food—take a tinned thought off the shelves of standardised mental fodder, because it is easier and quicker.

We find that a large mass of advertising is devised on the assumption that the public aimed at is vulgar, ignorant, irrational and at the mercy of its own simple desires. It may therefore be hazarded that any political party which relies on some of the professional propagandists whose work we have examined will in practice show many fascist characteristics, whatever platform it announces. A government, Left or Right, which shares with certain advertising experts an absolute contempt for the people it rules will be Nazi in essence. Goebbels once told E. A. Mowrer how he spent three days thinking out two words for a poster—'Always the National-Socialist agitator was warned to appeal to the mass, and to the lowest in the mass, not through the intellect but through the emotions, the instincts.' I do not share the contemptuous view but I do not think that the people of any nation could hold out against a permanent deprivation of reason and truth. A milder degree of dictation may be experienced if we get a government composed of business or political bosses, who will transfer to Westminster the habits acquired in Birmingham or the City or Transport House. Like Goebbels they will regard the public as a body to be doped into accepting their governmental policies, just as it was led into buying their insurance policies or patent medicines. The big trusts have helped to create a powerful machine for manipulating what is euphemistically termed public opinion, and it is easy to imagine it being used for sinister political purposes.

Advertising is a symptom, and cannot be treated as a

problem in itself. It is evidence that society suffers from an excessive development of competition for profit, to the frustration of other motives. The product of a lack of balance, it tends to make the lopsidedness worse. Government control can do a little—it ought after the war to check any advertising that stimulates the sale or consumption of luxury goods which could reasonably be made in small quantities but if sold in inflated volume will divert energy from the urgent work of physical reconstruction. But governments which learn the power of advertising will be tempted to use it to establish themselves as 'centre parties'. The remedy is not governmental but social control, and the need not for more laws and restrictions but for the control of publicity by society—a control exercised by individuals more responsible and aware of what is going on than many can be at present, and less disposed to let things slide and leave things to others.

REFERENCES TO CHAPTERS V & VI

1. *Week-end Review*, 1932.
2. Sidney and Beatrice Webb.
3. PEP Broadsheet, *Planning Post-War Industry*, No. 176, 2 September 1941.
4. *The Rape of the Masses*.
5. *The Economist*, 11 September 1937.
6. *Man and Society in an Age of Reconstruction*.
7. Messrs. Samson Clark's Bulletin, *The Radio Industry*.
8. *New Statesman*, 15 May 1937.
9. *Ibid*., Insurance Supplement, 23 May 1936.
10. *The Economist*, 21 August 1937.
11. *US*, No. 4, Bulletin of Mass-Observation.
12. *Change*, No. 2, 'Home Propaganda', Report prepared by Mass-Observation for the Advertising Service Guild.
13. Sir Kingsley Wood, *Spectator*, 19 November 1937.
14. Post Office Green Paper No. 8.

15. *Week-end Review*, 15 July 1933.
16. *Handbook* of the B.S.I., July 1940.
17. *Daily Telegraph*, 17 June 1938.
18. Published termly by the Sharnbrook Press, 140 Holland Road, W. 14.
19. F. E. Lumley, *The Propaganda Menace*.
20. *Germany Puts the Clock Back*.
21. *The House that Hitler Built*, 1937.

APPENDIX A

WE must not imagine that the advertisers are idle now, and most respectable papers contain these advertisements. For example, the *Observer* last Sunday had advertisements inviting us to wake up our liver bile with little liver pills in a way that would make us jump out of bed in the morning. *The Sunday Times*, in spite of the paper shortage, has a one-fifth of a page advertisement for Phyllosan, which 'revitalises the blood', whatever that means, 'fortifies the heart'—which sounds like the Minister of Information trying to keep up our morale, 'corrects our blood pressure' —unfortunately without any indication of how it does it, 'stimulates our metabolism' regardless of the fact that it is much more easily done by going for a gentle walk; 'strengthens our nerves', 'increases our vital forces'—quite meaningless phrases—but gives no indication whatever of the contents of the said remedy which is said to have all these effects on the system. The *Spectator*, complaining of the paper shortage, yet has half a page to give to an eye lotion which is specially recommended for Civil Defence workers when they return after an incident. I personally should have thought a dilute solution of boric acid would have been just as good, but it has the disadvantage of costing much less. The *News Chronicle* has an advertisement for Zambuk, an old friend, at the present moment specialising in relieving tired feet. (Prof. Hill went on to give the constituents of Zambuk, and discussed the merits of Bile Beans, Germolene, Limestone Phosphate, Yeast Vite and Beltona.)

Parliamentary Debates, House of Commons,
Official Report, 8 July 1941

APPENDIX B

MANKIND IN COUNCIL

A MESSAGE

1. To all of good-will, forgathered here to ease the burdens of a troubled world, we offer salutation and with a sense of fellowship pray humbly for the happiest of issues.

Civilisation itself stands at the cross-roads.

Shall this tremendous effort of the Nations go down in nothingness or shall it win to universal trust and understanding, blazing anew the trail of human hope, prosperity and freedom?

Too well we mark the crowding doubts, anxieties and fears, too well the whimperings of weakened faith, too well we realise the task.

But the divinity that glorifies great minds and souls and tries the courage and devotion of great hearts is never proved more truly than in extremity of trial.

Under Providence our faith lives on.

Beyond the patient sowing shall come the splendid reaping. Out of the day of travail shall come a new World-brotherhood of Man.

THE HOUSE OF HARRODS

(Whole page advert, *Observer*, 11 June 1933)

2. Now it is that a passionate urge comes on us to savour the 'green life' again. An urge that sends us roving on bridle paths and hillside, thankful with the birds that the drear dark days are safely overpast. And when in that lovely lassitude a day outdoors bestows, our * * * * seems good above all beers, let us remember that it too is part of Nature's rhythm. Barley and hops from our own rich earth

have made it, an elixir that runs like a golden thread through the humble pattern of our lives.

3. We have reached the shortest day. . . . Many of us have enough of the primeval sun-worship to make us feel that the day is worth marking. . . . The great tide of light has turned. Now it begins to flow again, slowly and imperceptibly, to the magnificent month when the whole of the longest working day is rounded by golden sunshine. The stellar rhythm is the master-wheel of all the activities of this Store. . . .

There is something sustaining in this vast recurrence. It may bring new needs and new duties, but it brings also the desire and the power to do them. It will lift a man to effort as the returning sea will lift a ship held in the shallows. It brings a cosmic instinct to the aid of will.

LIST OF BOOKS

A. S. J. BASTER, *Advertising Reconsidered*. (P. S. King.)

STUART CHASE, *Your Money's Worth*. (Cape.)

F. W. TAYLOR, *The Economics of Advertising*. (Allen & Unwin.)

F. R. LEAVIS and D. THOMPSON, *Culture and Environment*. (Chatto & Windus.)

D. THOMPSON, *Between the Lines*. (F. Muller.)

APPENDIX C

ADVERTISING IN WAR TIME

THOUGH many examples of post-1939 advertisements have been cited under earlier headings, this appendix is added to record some of the changes that the war caused in advertising and to state some of the objections that may be made against any commercial publicity in war time.

In the first year of war advertisements fitted in with, and perhaps helped to create, the feeling that things would go on much as usual while the blockade and internal revolution brought Germany to defeat. The pipe-holding vicars turned into padres, the haircream boys projected their smirks from under R.A.F. hats, the glamour girls joined the W.A.A.F. Advertising generally changed its tune to make the best use of situations offered by the war: 'Cigarette smokers are helping to win the economic war by smoking Turkish'; 'Buy a five-guinea suit for £4 and put the money saved to Defence Bonds'; 'As a help to the nation's purse— you should stick to beer. More than a hundred million pounds is likely to be collected in beer duty this year.' At the same time advertising was employed to bring to our notice new products alleged to be helpful in war time or to recommend new uses for existing lines. Petrol lamps, electric lighting sets, concrete shelters, first-aid outfits, disinfectants, and fire-extinguishers were the new necessities of life. Most of them represented a diversion of labour and energy from the war effort, some of them were useless for the advertised purpose; in reply to a question in the Commons it was stated that 'My right honourable friend is examining the possibilities of obtaining powers to prohibit the sale or advertisement of harmful preparations purporting to extinguish incendiary bombs' (*Official Report*, 1 July 1941).

In the early stages advertising urged us to indulge in

purchases which we now see to have been inappropriate under the circumstances. But the appeals did not cease when the goods became scarce. Cigarette advertisements were appearing during the worst shortage, in 1941, and when supplies improved we were regularly invited to buy X brand against other brands; and though it may be thought that such pressure is harmless it should be remembered that competitive advertising always increases the total demand for a product. *Any* cigarette advertisement, that is, means that more cigarettes are demanded—an increase hardly desirable in war time. In the same way many other things besides cigarettes continued to be advertised, when they were—or ought to have been—almost unobtainable. Of course numerous announcements contained the formula, 'Supplies are scarce: so go slow with ———.' Among these the instructions given for economising haircream were especially fatuous—'It is important to shake the bottle the right way, for "expert" shaking makes the cream "fluid".'

'Cashing in on the war effort' describes much of the advertising of the period. Naturally the patent medicines and proprietary foods hastened to demonstrate that we could not cope with overtime without a multi-vitamin pill (vitamin content unspecified), bring up our children without a proprietary oil, see in the blackout without a certain capsule. Firms the sale of whose products to private buyers was against the public interest attempted to exploit the circumstances of the time to ingratiate themselves with us. Beer advertisements appeared with an invitation to buy Savings Certificates, and later the brewers published under the heading 'What do I do if . . . ' instructions on how to behave in various war-time emergencies, with the label 'Space presented to the nation by . . . ' The Nuffield Organisation advertised the R.A.F. Benevolent Fund, and the 'Sunlight Window' printed the lay sermons of novelists. After a successful libel action against the Bishop of Birmingham the Cement Makers' Federation ran a series explaining why they advertised cement, with an oddly defensive 'Postscript for the Cynical'—'No, this doesn't mean merely the vociferation of a bunch of hard-boiled salesmen! It means making generally available the knowledge of experienced architects and engineers . . . ' etc.

There are various reasons why the interests concerned maintained what to many people seemed a superfluous activity. The Press had an eye to its profits, the advertising agents saw that if government departments ceased to advertise there would be small need for their services, firms which had invested large sums in purchasing reputations in peace desired to preserve that 'good-will' during war. The Advertising Association published a leaflet *The Function of Advertising in Wartime*, which concentrated on the last of the aims mentioned. There seems to have been some success in getting a favourable hearing from the government, if we may go by what Mr. Lyttelton said, when President of the Board of Trade, see p. 125.

It is noticeable that proprietary breads were allowed to continue in war time, and in some cases this may not have been on their merits. It is possible that a similar tenderness to firms with advertised reputations was shown in allowing the export to Canada of hundreds of tons of branded biscuits in 1941, at a time when biscuits had to be queued for in this country, and in the reserving of fruit for commercial jam makers.

One reason for the persistence of advertising in war time is revealed in a question put by Mr. Creech Jones in the Commons on 16 December 1941. He asked the Chancellor of the Exchequer if his attention had been drawn to

the costly advertising in national newspapers of goods which cannot be supplied in war time; that this expenditure deprives the nation . . . of large amounts which would otherwise be available for taxation; and whether he will take steps to prevent the advertising of goods which cannot be supplied and/or to prevent advertising, the object of which is, in fact, to evade taxation?

The Official Report continues:

> Sir K. Wood: In so far as my hon. Friend raises the question of taxation I would refer him to the reply I gave on 25th November last to my hon. Friend the Member for Newport (Sir R. Clarry). The other aspects of the question are matters for my right hon. Friends the President of the Board of Trade and the Minister of Supply.
>
> Mr. Creech Jones: Is the right hon. Gentleman aware of what appears to be systematic evasion by very expensive advertisements of articles which cannot possibly be supplied during the period of the war, and cannot something be done in order to stop that sort of evasion?

(Three other members put supplementary questions, one of them referring to 'one of the most flagrant examples of the gross waste of necessary raw materials', but no reply was given.)

There are three main objections to the continuance of displayed advertising in war time. First, on whatever grounds the exploitation of human qualities and failings may be defended in peace, it seems contemptible to take advantage of the hopes and fears, privation and heroism, which are associated with war. The reader may find his own epithets for the firm which capitalised the experience of men who drifted for days on a raft to push the merits of a dry battery which one of the sailors had carried.

Secondly, commercial advertising queers the pitch for government publicity. It is desirable that state departments should use advertising to popularise facilities, to explain regulations and see that they are carried out, so long as there is a free Press and an alert Parliament to take the opportunity of criticising such advertising and see that it does not become a cloak for policies not accepted by the electors. But it can hardly be doubted that government advertising during the war has been weakened by the commercial matter that flanks it in the Press. The commercial compete with governmental announcements not only by being there at all, but also by simulating the style of official advertising. A maker of toilet paper exhibits top-left in his advert the Royal Arms and follows with official-sounding copy in a formal type; a Rawlplug advertisement reproduces the whole of a Builders' campaign advertisement as its heading, putting the words 'Ministry of Works' under the reproduction; anti-aircraft guns head an advertisement that starts like a recruiting campaign for the R.A.F. or the W.A.A.F. and ends by recommending Gillette razors. An interesting Report (*Change*, No. 2) prepared by Mass-Observation for the Advertising Service Guild says that 'there is some danger of the public becoming considerably confused between what are official and what are unofficial instructions'.

The Ministry of Food has consistently tried by well-written, straightforward advertisements to educate the consumer in the theory and practice of the diet necessary to maintain good health; and it has had some success. But this would have been greater had there been no counter-barrage from proprietary foods and patent medicines. They continue to propagate misleading information, as in peace time; but in war time the practice is more objectionable because rationing and restricted choice make it unlikely that an unplanned diet will supply the essentials. Typically, a pill claiming to contain all the known vitamins with iron, calcium and phosphorus is alleged to provide 'a quick and simple way to better health'.

A third objection to advertising in time of war is the waste of paper involved. The Government announced that paper was an essential war material and should not be wasted, but though it prohibited the sending of circulars and unsolicited catalogues (except for books and seeds) it did nothing to fix the ratio of advertisements that a newspaper or magazine might contain. Thus tons of paper—probably 18,000 tons a year for prestige advertising in periodicals other than newspapers—are consumed in puffing unobtainable or scarce products. Few periodicals followed the example of the *New Statesman* in cutting down displayed announcements to a small uniform size—a possible means incidentally of removing the unfair advantage that the merely wealthy advertiser has in peace time. This waste of paper continued at a time when books were going out of print and publishers were hard pressed to get supplies. What a great difference would be made by a diversion from advertising is shown by the fact that an average displayed advertisement in one day's issue of a million sale journal would yield enough paper for 5,000 copies of a medium length book. Half a dozen superfluous advertisements in the 'national' Press could have been made into 170,000 books. It cannot of course be assumed that paper released by cutting down advertisements would necessarily be available for books.

In short, commercial advertising in war is a misuse of labour and material needed for other purposes; it distracts public attention from concerns which people should follow closely for their own interest; it converts what should be savings into expenditure on goods and services which the country cannot afford.

INDEX

217